U S Import   10.99

CW00539175

Form, cast out of time,
is home for the sacred Light.
Kneel. A child is born.

--Haiku by Dusty Bunker

Quintiles and Tredeciles

The Geometry of the Goddess

Dusty Bunker

Whitford Press

1469 Morstein Road
West Chester, Pennsylvania 19380 U.S.A.

Quintiles and Tredeciles: The Geometry of the Goddess
by Dusty Bunker

Copyright © 1989 by Dusty Bunker

All rights reserved. No part of this work may be reproduced or used in any form or by any means--graphic, electronic, or mechanical, including photocopying, mimeographing, recording, taping or information storage and retrieval systems--without written permission from the copyright holder.

Library of Congress Card Number: 89-51667
International Standard Book Number: 0-914918-98-2

Manufactured in the United States of America

Published by Whitford Press,
A division of
Schiffer Publishing, Ltd.
1469 Morstein Road
West Chester, Pennsylvania 19380
Please write for a free catalog.
This book may be purchased from the publisher.
Please include $2.00 postage.
Try your bookstore first.

Contents

Introduction   7

In the Beginning   13

Part I: Aspects Revealed

Chapter 1: The Numbers   15

Chapter 2: The Vesica Piscis and the Divine Triangle   31

Chapter 3: The Quintile and Tredecile Explained   49

Chapter 4: 36, the Decile: The Oath of Secrecy   61

Footnotes   69

Part II: Aspects Delineated

Quintile and Tredecile Chart and Definition   73

Forty Astrological Charts as Examples (with Biographies)   81

Personality Compilations by Aspect   163

Sources of Charts   179

Footnotes   180

Suggested Reading List   181

This book is dedicated to the Light.

Introduction

When I was five years old, an incident occurred that changed my life. Although it happens to all early school children, this event had a profound and lasting impact on me. I learned to read. This story will be told at the appropriate time in this book. The point is that this spiritual experience never was explained to my satisfaction through examining my natal astrological chart. I have wondered about this missing link since I began studying metaphysics in general and astrology in particular.

On November 2, 1987, around 10 in the morning, while riding home from our cabin on Conner Pond in the hills of New Hampshire, I found my answer. (See chart on page 8.) It was a moment of intense emotional contact with the roots of my consciousness. The pieces became the whole. That moment of revelation opened the door to another cupboard filled with rare ingredients. It was my turn to cry "Eureka!"

And I did. At that point, my husband, comfortable with my idiosyncratic manner of dealing with life, merely smiled and asked, "Now what?" Since he is used to waking at 2:30 A.M. and finding me on my hands and knees, in the dark, bent over an array of books with

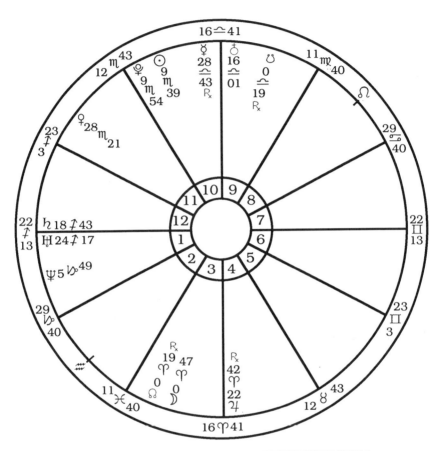

EUREKA: QUINTILE AND TREDECILE IDEA
NOVEMBER 2, 1987 10 A.M. E.S.T.
ROCHESTER, N.H.
43N18 70W59
TROPICAL--PLACIDUS

a flashlight, he takes much of my behavior in stride.

However, back in the car, using information I had gathered through numerology; sacred geometry; masonic, religious and Egyptian symbology; and astrology, my moment of Eureka revealed the intense importance of the little-used or understood aspect of 72 degrees--the quintile--and its partner, a 108-degree aspect, which I then temporarily had called the tritile.

My experience with the 108-degree aspect was the result of studying and exploring sacred geometry with a protractor, compass, and ruler along with the compilation of information gleaned from many texts (including an old masonic manuscript) mixed with studying astrological charts and sprinkled with hours of pencil chewing as I gazed into space. This aspect explained something I felt so profoundly in the depths of my being that I knew it should have shown in my natal chart. But I was not aware of it until I realized, through the exercise of the above-mentioned disciplines, the importance of this aspect.

I thought about this aspect for many months and, as fate would have it, I happened to sit next to Steven McFadden, another astrologer and New Hampshirite, on our plane trip home from the Welcome to the Planet Earth conference in Oregon in the summer of 1988. As is my habit when working on new material, I do not discuss it much because I believe in the old teaching: "to know, to do, to dare and to be silent." For me, excessive discussion dissipates the energy. But Steven is an unusual man, and I found myself telling him about my new manuscript. He was intrigued and said he would think about what I had said.

Some days later, Steven called me. He had come across the 108-degree aspect that is called the tredecile, trecile or sesquiquintile. It is considered a minor aspect.

The quintile and tredecile were considered minor, but from all my research, the indications were that these were major aspects considering the impact they have on our lives and on the life of the planet. And I knew that I had substantial proof to back up this claim.

I would like to reprint a letter I received from Steven a few days after our phone conversation because he makes some points so beautifully that his message would suffer in my paraphrasing.

Dear Dusty:

Shortly after saying good-bye to you and hanging up the phone yesterday, I set out to run a couple of miles. As I ran I recognized that the quintile in my chart from the Ascendant to Pluto, and the [tredecile] [1] from Chiron to Pluto formed a planetary picture similar to a T-square or an easy opposition. After all, my Chiron and Ascendant are opposed to each other, and related again through Pluto.

So as I ran, I contemplated this picture and what it might mean. I also thought a lot about Pluto down there, deep in my Fourth House. Being an aggressive Capricorn, I determined to do everything I could to awaken the Plutonic force and bring it into the world in a balanced way. And then I remembered that little passage from Marc Edmund Jones about the quintile entitling the native to make "demands of cooperation or spiritual help from the universe."

Right on, I thought. *I'll demand help in activating Pluto.*

Then, just as I let that thought build in intensity and clarity, my right foot stubbed a rock and I tumbled ass over moustache into the road.

In nine years of running, the only other time I have fallen was a winter day when I was chugging along contemplating what a fine person I was. The lesson that day was clear: Pride goeth before a fall. The lesson yesterday, I believe, was equally clear: Marc Edmund Jones was wrong. We may ask of God or the Universe, and the quintile may ensure that the requests of such fortunate natives get special attention; but the whole notion of "demand" is a twisted perception of how the universe maintains harmony and balance.

The more I think about it, the more it seems the action of "demanding" is ultra macho or masculine--certainly not in keeping with the feminine geometry of the quintile or (tredecile) as you have described, and certainly not, at least in my case, the way to go about activating Pluto.

I wanted to share this story with you so that if you choose to repeat the quintile description from Jones, you can offer another perspective. Demands do not make for a balanced person, a balanced relationship, or a balanced universe.

I remain,
Chastened but cheerful,
Steven

I laughed out loud when reading this letter. I could picture Steven with his full moustache tumbling tail over tea kettle, and I loved his description of his humanness to which, I am sure, we can all relate. I also was grateful for his insights.

At any rate, because I feel there is overwhelming proof that the quintile and tredecile should be considered more important in astrological charts, I am offering the information in this book to you with, I must say, considerable trepidation. But I take heart from the renowned astrologer, Carl Payne Tobey, who once wrote: "Our greatest fear is that students will accept only what we have done till now and then get into a rut." [2]

What is true of all new information is that it must work for you. Indeed, the proof is in the pudding. So please, try these ideas. Perhaps the aroma or the taste will satiate some of your cravings and then motivate you to open the door to your cupboard of alchemical ingredients. Your magic cauldron is bubbling and waiting, so choose your spices. Ready...set...EUREKA!

In the Beginning

There is a thing confusedly formed,
Born before Heaven and Earth.
Silent and void
It stands alone and does not change,
Goes round and does not weary.
It is capable of being the mother of the world.... [1]

"The Cosmic Egg from which the sun, Ra, was hatched was laid by the Nile Goose:...The egg also signifies the yoni." [2]

Yoni. "Vulva," the primary Tantric object of worship symbolized variously by a triangle, fish, double-pointed oval, horseshoe, egg, fruits, and so forth.

The Yoni Yantra or triangle was known as the Primordial Image, representing the Great Mother as source of all life. As the genital focus of her divine energy, the Tantra was adored as a geometrical symbol, as the cross was adored by Christians. [3]

Mother Goose originated in ancient Egypt, where she was Mother Hathor, incarnate in the Nile Goose. She laid the golden egg of the sun, another way of saying she gave birth to Ra. His solar disc was sometimes called the Goose-egg. Some Egyptian writings called the goose Creatress of the World because she produced the whole universe in a primordial World Egg. [4]

"Zero also represents the Cosmic Egg...." [5]

"Ten or twenty billion years ago...all the matter and energy in the universe was concentrated at extremely high density--a kind of cosmic egg, reminiscent of the creation myths of many cultures--perhaps into a mathematical point with no dimensions at all." [6]

"...the one huge mass at the beginning [is] the 'cosmic egg' because out of it the cosmos was formed." [7]

In the beginning, the feminine principle was seen as the fundamental cosmic force. All ancient peoples believed that the world was created by a female Deity. This Goddess was conceived as bringing the universe into being either alone or in conjunction with a male consort, usually Her son, whom the Goddess created parthenogenetically.[8] Procreation was not understood to be connected with coitus, and it was thought that woman--like the Goddess--brought forth life alone and unaided. [9]

Part I: Aspects Revealed

Chapter 1
The Numbers

Tao generates one. One generates two. Two generates three. Three generates all things. [1]

Ancient initiates and avatars viewed numbers from a different perspective than we do today. Their science of numbers had no relationship to the mathematics we currently use. If we are to understand the teachings of the ancient mystery schools, especially those taught through numbers and sacred geometry-- which are the basis of the proof offered in this book for the validations of the quintile and the tredecile--then we need to examine the way in which these ancient initiates thought about and used numbers.

To these early people, a number was the "extreme reduction of philosophic thought" which explained the formative life process. Each number was a universal law that emerged from the preceding number, and all numbers emerged from the One. The orderly progression of the numbers resulted in time and space and form, and the dissolution of that form which was then recycled and reborn. "...in the ancient temple civilization of Egypt, numbers, our most ancient form of symbol, did not simply designate quantities but instead were considered to be concrete definitions of energetic formative principles of nature." [2]

Therefore, there was a distinction between figures and numbers.

Figures were used to measure how far, how many, and how soon whereas numbers represented precise formative principles in nature. Esoterically, Two was not the result of One plus One but rather the result of the emerging of creative energy from the One.

Also, Two was not division of the One. If a single-cell fetus divided, it would grow no bigger. Rather, it would divide into smaller parts.

Two was not addition; it was multiplication: the One multiplied or generated into the Two. This awareness may have resulted from observation of the birth process that showed that a cosmic hand did not reach out of the heavens and present the adult female with a child to care for. Instead, the woman's body began to expand, like the expanding universe, and at some point another being emerged from her body. The woman multiplied into the Mother and the Child. Out of the One came the Two. It was an emerging process.

Also, when the ancients worked with multiplication, their calculations were related directly to both metaphysical and natural life processes. "Schwaller de Lubicz called this mode the 'principle of crossing.' [Interestingly, we continue to symbolize multiplication with the sign of the cross: X]. This crossing was...a symbol for the process by which things enter into corporeal existence. All birth into nature requires a crossing of opposites." [3] This "principle of crossing" will be referred to when we examine the divine triangle.

We can see that wo/man viewed numbers as the embodiment of the progressive universal law of life rather than a quantitative assessment of objects. This important distinction will serve as the basis for the information to be presented here.

To explain number as the origin of all things, we can examine the Zero and the numbers One through Nine as the framework of all number interpretation. All principles are contained within these ten entities, and since every combination of numbers beyond Nine reduces or adds to a single number, a thorough knowledge of the meaning of the Zero and the numbers One through Nine is all that is needed to examine any multiple number. Multiple numbers reflect a joining of the principles contained within each single number.

In this book, we will concentrate on the numbers One through Five because they are the ones that are involved in the proof offered to substantiate the quintile and the tredecile. Anyone interested in researching and studying numerology more thoroughly can refer to the suggested reading list at the back of this book.

Lao-tzu, the Chinese philosopher and reputed founder of Taoism, wrote: "Tao generates one. One generates two. Two generates three. Three generates all things." Tao is that in which all things exist and happen.

Since it was universally accepted before 1,000 B.C. that the Great Mother conceived the entire universe in Her cosmic egg and gave birth to all that "is, was, and ever shall be," we can combine these two terms--Tao and the Cosmic Egg of the Great Mother--for perhaps a clearer picture of the sequential unfolding from the Zero.

Zero: The Tao, the Cosmic Egg of the Great Mother, is that in which all things exist and happen. It is all that is, was, and ever shall be.

> At some particular time in the past, then, all the matter and energy of the universe must have existed in one large lump. At that time in the past ("zero-time") the universe could not possibly have been as it appears today; the Universe-we-know could only have existed since this zero-time and this zero-time can in fact be considered the beginning of our Universe. [4]

The Cosmic Egg is all the matter and energy in the universe concentrated "into a mathematical point with no dimensions at all." Zero means no thing. "It is misleading to describe the expansion of the universe as a sort of distending bubble viewed from the outside. By definition, nothing we can ever know about *was* outside." [5] Zero is the "zero-time" when the universe was "one large lump," the Cosmic Egg.

Life begins in the womb, that spherical shape that is the most divine part of us, having the ability to create Life. We become co-creators with the Great Mother. This is the Cosmic Egg in which the

Universe was conceived and in which it was born.

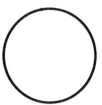

Tao/Cosmic Egg generates One: One is unity and could be symbolized by the circle because it is united and whole or One. One also may have symbolized woman as representative of the Great Mother here on earth who contained wholeness or unity in that she carried the human egg just as the Great Mother carried the Cosmic Egg or the Zero energy from which all is born. Herein lies the potential for unfolding.

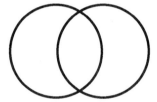

One generates Two: A circle merging from a circle in two equal and connected parts is a symbol for the Two. Since we understand that the ancients did not view Two as the addition of One and One but rather saw the Two emerging from the One, we can relate this concept to the Mother giving birth to the child. From the One emerged the Two. The image of the two overlapping circles will figure importantly in the proof for the importance and validity of the quintile and tredecile.

The closest thing to divinity was the ability to bring forth life. Therefore, it was natural to view woman as the great Mother's microcosmic image on earth. The Great Mother gave birth to the Universe; the human mother gave birth to the child.

In two, polarity takes form. We begin to understand the interrelationships we must experience with other things in our world. Two implies awareness through opposites. The Yin and Yang are born.

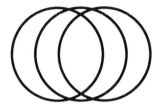

Two generates Three: With Three, time was born. The child, representative of the human race, was observed to go through three stages of growth: infancy, adulthood, and old age. Past, present, and future with its accompanying birth, life, and death became a linear reality upon which the world of nature was built. Three became the trinity in all major religions, reflecting the concept of the process of birth, life, and death inherent in nature.

At this point, the Three does not incorporate the physical mother and child but the potential for that growth. The Three-in-One concept behind all trinities is the idea that within the One is the creative energy of the Three that will subsequently generate life.

The triangle has long been a religious symbol of the trinity.

> In ancient societies and in some contemporary ones, it is recognized as the trinity of the Goddess, signifying the Goddess in her three forms--Maiden, Mother, Crone. The triangle was the Egyptian hieroglyphic symbol for woman. In the Greek alphabet, the symbol for delta is the triangle, signifying the Holy Door, vulva of the All-Mother-Demeter ("Mother Delta")....The triangle represented the Virgin Moon Goddess called Men-Nefer, archaic deity of the first Mother-city of Memphis.

> The triangle symbolizes a gathering of universal creative energy as can be seen in the Great Pyramid which is considered to be a giant electrical conductor, an accumulator of creative energy awaiting release.

> In 1859, Werner von Siemens, founder of the German electrical company by the same name, climbed to the top of the Great Pyramid and stuck his finger into the air over his head in a triumphant gesture. To his great surprise, he

received a prickling sensation through his finger and also heard a sharp noise.

Curious by nature, he wrapped a wet paper around the metal neck of a wine bottle to create a crude Leyden jar, a device for storing an electric charge. As he held the device above his head, sparks began shooting out of the Leyden jar. It appeared to von Siemens that the Great Pyramid was an electrical conductor of some sort, a focus of creative energy.

Some esoteric historians believe the Great Pyramid was not the tomb of a pharaoh but...an initiation temple. Here the candidate for initiation was laid in the granite sarcophagus for three-and-one-half days while the Ka, the soul of the initiate, travelled the Universe gathering information and experience necessary for qualification as an adept....

The cone-shaped hats of witches and wizards are a solidified triangle. Was this their way of drawing in the universal energy to enhance their feats of magic, of working with the natural forces of the Earth to bring about physical change?

Remember the stereotypical picture of a child who has not learned her/his lessons or is considered "stupid," sitting on a stool in the corner and wearing a dunce's cap? The dunce's hat is cone-shaped....

Church steeples are exaggerated triangles, reaching high into the heavens as if to draw upon cosmic consciousness....

In handwriting analysis, triangular or wedge-shaped strokes indicate people who are energetic and daring.... [6]

Three generates all things: The aim of analysis is to split up a thing or an idea until it is reduced to an irreducible element. One thus reaches magnitudes such that each of them can only be defined by two other magnitudes. This is the original "trinity."

The idea here is that a "thing" such as time, when reduced to its irreducible elements--past, present, and future--can only be defined when one definition is related to the other two. For example, we know present because of past and future.

Growth or nature unfolds in three dimensions. Space and time as we know them are triple. Space, which can only be defined by the objects within it, is described as "the unlimited or indefinitely great three-dimensional expanse in which all material objects are located and all events occur." [7]

Time is "the system of those sequential relations that any event has to any others, as past, present, or future...." [8] The essence of time and space is triple.

This may be why the ancient Chinese considered the number One to have the same value as the Three. It seems that the ancient Egyptians held this belief as well. The idea of divinity as the Three-in-One, or the triangle in the circle, takes on new meaning when viewed in this light.

The common expression, "Things happen in threes," embodies the metaphysical principle that Three generates all things and that nature unfolds in three dimensions. One might wonder why we subliminally have chosen Three as the quantity that things happen in rather than Two or Eight. With a knowledge of numbers such as we have discussed above, one begins to understand that we did not choose this number arbitrarily. The choice emerges from a deep knowledge that numbers represent principles and qualities that remain unchanging. Numbers are truth.

We can examine a few important units in life to see how Three, the most creative number, is the principle upon which nature is built and is worthy of its selection as the symbol of adoration by religious groups all over the world.

All colors can be produced from red, yellow, and blue, the three basic colors. Music is composed of three parts: rhythm, tone, and harmony. Sir Isaac Newton (1642-1727) formulated the three laws of motion. "Nearly all subsequent mechanics have been based upon his conclusions, and it is really astonishing to note how often the most recondite analyses in this field turn out to be only reaffirmations of his principles." [9]

In phonetics, the study of speech sounds, there are three points: "the place of production, the means of transmission, and the place of reception." [10] There are three important aspects of a sound wave: amplitude, frequency and phase.

As stated before, our dimension is determined by breadth,

width, and length; time is measured by the past, present, and future. The human family is composed of mother, father, and child.

Three is a basic division in the creation of nature, symbolized by the equilateral triangle (three equal sides), the first perfect form that can be constructed with straight lines. This triangle as the trinity is honored in most cultures as the divine family--Mother, Father, Child--an exoteric or outward expression of an esoteric or hidden truth.

The trinity has been expressed in multifaceted ways throughout history and in differing cultures, but it always maintained the integrity of the Three. In Mother Goddess worship, it is the Maiden, Mother, and Crone, the three aspects of the Triple Goddess. This represents time in that the obvious stages of a woman's life are youth (the Maiden), maturity (the Mother), and old age (the Crone). It also represents the three phases of the Moon (new, full, and old).

The Riddle of the Sphinx embodied this trinitarian principle of time when it asked what walked on four feet in the morning, two feet at noon, and three feet in the evening. The answer is a human who crawls during infancy, walks upright during adult years and uses a cane in old age.

The time concepts of past, present, and future also are signified by the Hindu trinity that is said to be a modern adaptation of the Triple Goddess: Brahma (the Creator), Vishnu (the Preserver), and Shiva (the Transformer or Destroyer).

In Tantric Buddhism, the downward-pointing triangle was held in the same reverence as the Christian cross and the Jewish Star of David are today. It was called the Yoni, and it represented the genital area of the Great Mother from which She gave birth to the entire universe. Since all observation of nature proved that the female of all species gives birth mysteriously out of her body, the female became the representative of the Great Mother, copying Her macrocosmic magic on a microcosmic level.

As mentioned earlier, the Great Mother gave birth to the universe; the human mother gave birth to the child. That child experienced three stages in life: youth, adulthood, and old age. The passage of time (past, present, and future) was symbolized by the three sides of the Great Mother's Yoni.

Similarly, we can find the symbolism of the Three in the name Solomon, which always has stood for wisdom. In Hebrew gematria, where each letter of the alphabet has a numerical counterpart, the name Solomon adds to 180, ideally the number of degrees in the arc of the sun from sunrise to sunset, the period of light. Light is a symbol of awareness. Solomon, or Sol-Om-On in three phases, represents the rising, peaking, and setting sun, again punctuating the idea that with the passage of time, the light of wisdom is possible.

There were a number of Solomons in history, such as Salmanu from Babylonia. The Solomons of Babylonia presided over temples dedicated to "divine wisdom"--or we might say these temples were dedicated to divine Light. The Tower of Babel was one such edifice.

Religions were built upon the cycles of nature. Nature provided daily proof of the creative aspects of the division of the One, the circle or wholeness or unity. Three is the most creative of the numbers because it is the crucible of life, the cauldron in which the Three parts of nature are alchemically mixed.

Therefore, the original trinity or the triangle embodies the concepts of time (past, present, future/birth, life, death) and space (length, width, and depth). It is *in* time, the Three, that all things happen. It is from this Three-in-One principle that the Four (or form, symbolized by the square) emerges.

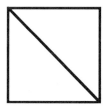

Four: Four is the square; the square is a symbol of form--the physical body and the material world.

For two millennia we in the Judeo-Christian tradition have been taught that we should deny the physical and attain to the spiritual. The Western philosophy of denying the pleasures of the physical world for some greater reward in a celestial realm where everything is wonderful and pure and full of Light is reflected in what some numerologists have written about the Four. Four is a drudge and a burden and can only be endured; Four does not easily find happiness and joy; Four is dull, uninteresting, and uninspired; and so forth. These qualities are not listed as the negative side of the number but seem to be stressed as the crux of the number.

What this attitude does is deny the Spirit in matter. It denies the spiritual process of nature with the magical play of light over the equator that creates the seasons. It denies the existence of the soul of the Earth. It separates us from nature--and in the process we have become spiritual paupers.

In the recent PBS series hosted by Bill Moyers called "The Power of Myth," Joseph Campbell told the story of an oriental sage speaking to a group of westerners about their belief system. "God against man, man against God, man against nature, nature against man, nature against God. What a funny religion."

To the ancients, nature or matter was the container or the repository of the Life Force. Matter contained the Light. Matter was Spirit made manifest, or solidified Light. There was no distinction or separation between nature and our Maker while in the physical body.

This knowing parallels today's scientific theory that our physical bodies are composed of the debris of stars that exploded millions of years ago; we are literally star children or solidified Light.

As a result, the number Four, the number of Mother Earth and its corporeal pleasures that have been connected with the female, have come down to us as something "spiritual" people avoid and shun, and others relegated to the back rooms. No wonder Freud had such a heyday with the frustrated sexual energies of his Victorian period.

If people tell you that the number Four is grossly material, dull and uninspired, a drudge and a complainer, ask them how they feel about sex and food, an eagle on the wind and daffodils in the spring, snowflakes on the windowpane and the birth of a child.

The sacred Four emerges from the Three. As mentioned above, its symbol is the square and it rules the physical world of form. Out of the nine numbers, it is the only number that determines equal value in the surface and circumference of a circle and a square or, symbolically, it is the only value that determines form.

For example: a square with sides four inches each measures sixteen inches in circumference (4+4+4+4=16) and sixteen inches in area or surface (4 X 4=16). A circle with a diameter of four inches measures π 4 in circumference. The formula for the circumference of a circle is C= π d, d being the diameter. This same circle measure π 4 in area. The formula for the area of a circle is A= π r 2. R is the radius or half the diameter, which here would be half of four or two. When squaring r or two we have four. The formula then reads A= π 4.

Four is the only number that determines equal value in the area and circumference of a circle and a square. Remember that the ancients saw number as a philosophical reduction of principles, so that this uniqueness of the Four indicated that Spirit (the circle) and matter (the square) were one in the same, having equal value.

Four has obvious associations with the Earth in terms of the four corners of the Earth (even though the Earth is spherical), the four winds, the four points on the compass, the four seasons, and so on. And what about eating a "square" meal?

As a child I wondered about many things, like why meals were called "square" when the dinner plates were round. Why didn't we call them three round meals a day? As a student of sacred geometry and numbers, I now understand that the expression is symbolic because the square gives substance, solidity, nourishment to the physical body (the body is one expression of the square symbol).

So, Three gives rise to the Four, the world of form. Time creates the four seasons; the three dimensions construct the world of matter; the three primary colors create all the hues; the three parts of music compose the sonata, and so forth.

See the accompanying chart entitled The Four Elements, the building blocks of life, which is taken from my earlier book, *Numerology, Astrology and Dreams*. It is reproduced here on page 26. It lists a number of well-known divisions of Four related to the four elements: Fire, Water, Air, and Earth.

The four-part name of our Maker, the Tetragrammaton, is known as Jod-Heh-Vau-Heh. This is the aspect of the Creator that operates in the physical world because it rules the seasons, without which there is no life.

THE FOUR ELEMENTS
The Building Blocks of Life

THEIR EXPRESSION IN THE PHYSICAL WORLD

Elements	Fire	Water	Air	Earth
Seasons	Spring	Summer	Fall	Winter
Tarot suits	Wands	Cups	Swords	Pentacles
Playing card suits	Clubs	Hearts	Spades	Diamonds
Tetragammatron	Jod	Heh	Vau	Heh
Sacred Trapezoid	10	5	6	5
Serpent signs	Leo	Scorpio	Aquarius	Taurus
Astrological types	ardent	emotional	intellectual	practical
Apostles	Mark	John	Matthew	Luke
World myth figures (i.e., Sphinx)	lion	eagle	woman	bull
Nature spirits (Paracelsus)	salamander	undines	sylphs	gnomes
Greek philosophical qualities	morality	aesthetics	intellect-uality	physicality
Human	spirit	soul	mind	body
Human functions (Jung)	intuition	feeling	thinking	sensation
Human bodies	vital/ etheric	emotional/ astral	mental/ causal	physical

Through gematria, the number values of Jod-Heh-Vau-Heh are 10-5-6-5, which are used to construct the Sacred Trapezoid.

(See diagram on page 65) This trapezoid shows the relationship between the earth tipped at its 23 1/2-degree angle to the ecliptic (the path it travels around the sun). Without this polar tip, we would not have the play of the sun over the equator (and therefore there would be no seasons and no life as we know it).

There were other names for the Creator, but this is the one that is directly related to the physical world and everyday life. Jod-Heh-Vau-Heh, or IHVH, JHVH, YHVH, or Jehovah is that part of the Creator in the physical plane. It is the stuff in which we live and move and have our being. Nature is spiritual. The Four is Spirit in matter.

Five: Five is nature or life itself. This is the quickening that takes place in form. Form (or Four) itself is not "alive" in the sense we know it until the quickening takes place. Four determines form; Five imbues the form with life. When this happens, the Four gives birth to the Five.

Five is called the keystone in the arch of life because it is the central number in the cosmic blueprint represented by the numbers One through Nine.

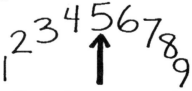

The symbol for Five is the pentagram, whose five points are a stylized replica of wo/man with her/his arms outstretched. It also has been called the pentangle, pentalpha, Devil's Sign, Witches' Cross, Wizard's Star, Goblin's Cross, Witches' Foot, Star of Knowledge, and Pentacle of the Virgin. It was used by the Pythagoreans and other philosophers, witches, and magicians.

The pentagram represents the five senses with which the human being is endowed. Five always has been recognized as the pivotal point in cycles when a change in the physical will occur. Of course, the most elementary change in the physical is when the soul enters or leaves the body.

Five is the quickening. In early cultures it generally was accepted that the soul did not enter the fetus until the fifth month of pregnancy, therefore the fetus could be aborted prior to this time without punishment.

Prior to 1869, the Catholic church's Doctrine of Passive Conception concurred with this belief, and again, abortion prior to the fifth month was not considered a crime.

Before the fifth month, the fetus was a form, number Four, without the life breath, the soul, that entered through the Five. This idea was prevalent throughout many cultures at that time.

There is an "old wive's tale" (the old wife is the Crone in the Mother Goddess religion, revered for her wisdom) that says illnesses turn for better of worse in the fifth hour, fifth day, or fifth week.

Our five senses are highlighted under this number, which can be shown by the symbolic choice of the apple in many cultures as the epitome of knowledge. If you slice an apple horizontally, you will find five seeds in the shape of a pentagram. It was when Adam ate the apple that Eve picked that they took on conscious awareness through their five senses.

The apple is a symbol of knowledge in many cultures. The Druids had seven sacred trees, one of which was the apple tree. In Greek mythology the daughters of the night, the four Hesperides, guarded the golden apples which grew in a sumptuous garden at the edge of the world. Today we give an apple, rather than a plum or pomegranate, to the teacher.

When Eve and Adam took of the apple, change occurred (the Five) and they had to leave their heavenly abode (the Three-in-One) to enter the world of form (the Four).

Ancient philosophers and alchemists often used the five-pointed star to symbolize the human being as a miniature replica of the greater life pattern of the cosmos. The number Five represented life.

The builders of the Great Pyramid used the number Five, the number of life, as their measure. The pyramid is constructed on the inch and the sacred cubit. The pyramid inch is one 500-millionth part of the earth's polar axis (the axis is the only straight or true measure since the Earth's surface is an irregular sphere).

One inch was used by Egyptian initiates to indicate the 365 1/4 days in the solar year. Thus it has been possible to measure thousands of years of history on a time line that runs through the Great Pyramid. The sacred cubit is 25 inches or one 20-millionth part of the earth's polar axis.

Also, the original perimeter of the base of the pyramid was 36,524 inches, or one hundred times the number of days in a solar tropical year. This means that each side measures 9,131 inches.

Hidden in these stone measurements is the value of π, the standard measure of the relationship between the circumference and the diameter of a circle, a value so sacred it was hidden in the first name of the Creator in the Bible. ALHIM in Hebrew gematria reduces to 3.1415, the value of π.

The height of the pyramid is to twice its base as one is to 3.1415 or π. This formula is written as:

5813:2 X 9131 :: 1:3.1415+

The sarcophagus in the main chamber was constructed upon the same π proportions: its height is to twice its base as one is to 3.1415.

The Great Pyramid, a mathematical stone message, is a monument to the number Five, the number of life. It incorporates celestial and terrestrial measurements in its architecture, and these cycles measure the mystery of life, the relationship between time and the eternal.

Five is the number of change because it represents nature or life, which is in a constant state of flux. One of the laws of physics is that the only constant is change. This is the law of Five--the law of life.

This has been a very brief introduction into the meaning of the first five numbers, those used in this text to explain and substantiate the importance of the quintile and the tredecile.

For in-depth information on numbers, see the suggested reading list at the end of this book.

Chapter 2
The Vesica Piscis and the Divine Triangle

It will be found that some of the most important features of God's creation are inextricably built around the precise geometrical relation of a square and a circle.... [1]

The square is composed of two triangles.

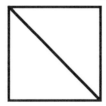

The first two so-called perfect forms in geometry are the triangle and the square because they are the first two visible shapes that can be constructed with straight lines. We will further explore the geometric and philosophic meaning of the triangle (the Three), and the square (the Four), because, according to the ancients, they are the basis upon which life was created.

These are also the geometrical shapes and the values used in constructing the Divine Triangle of Pythagorean theorem fame. We shall discover how the Pythagorean right triangle with the classic values of 3, 4, and 5 is the original trinity upon which the world was created and upon which world religions are based. This information was the ultimate secret taught at all the ancient mystery schools.

Although Pythagoras (circa 580 B.C.) brought this triangle to our attention, it was well known long before his time. A clay tessera (token) from about 2,000 B.C., upon which this 3-4-5 triangle was inscribed, was found in an Egyptian tomb.

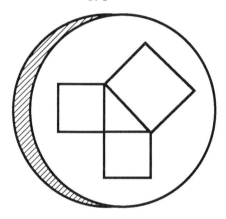

We shall see how this right triangle (as seen in the clay tessera) substantiates the 72-degree quintile and the 108-degree tredecile.

However, in the beginning was the Vesica Piscis, as seen below.

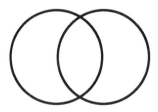

The Vesica Piscis is described as "an upright oval or **almond** shape often surrounding a sacred figure; it is produced by two intersecting circles and is a basic figure in sacred geometry. See also MANDORLA"[2]

The mandorla is "the vesica piscis, or ichthus, the almond-shaped aureole, the 'mystical almond' which depicts divinity; holiness; the sacred; virginity, the vulva. It also denotes an opening or gateway and the two sides represent the opposite poles and all duality." [3]

Another definition reads: "an elliptical figure in pointed form, usually one made by the intersection of two arcs and used, esp. in early Christian art, as an emblem of Christ; mandorla." [4]

In Chapter 1 I mentioned that the Yoni, the Great Mother's genital area through which all life is born, is described as the vulva, the primary Tantric object of worship symbolized variously by a triangle, fish, double-pointed oval, horseshoe, eggs....

The Vesica Piscis (as seen on this page) is the upright double-pointed oval that depicts divinity and the vulva (the female genital area), and it also denotes an opening or gateway with its two sides embodying the principle of duality. In these descriptions we can see a developing picture of the Vesica Piscis as the female vulva, the opening or gateway through which life emerges.

Virginity also is associated with the Vesica Piscis. The original meaning of the word "virgin" was an independent woman. It had nothing to do with her sexual activity. The early patriarchs tried to "clean up" the birth process by removing the sensuality of the sex act and proclaiming a virgin as a woman who had no sexual relations and therefore was "untainted" by physical desire. The old Mother Goddess religion approved of sensual pleasure; the new Father God religion disapproved of sensual pleasure. Other cultures were in tune with the earthiness of the birth process of the Great Mother.

One can only marvel at the patriarchal interpretations of the emotional experience of the people who created these figures (seen on page 34). On page 34, the figure of "Tlazolteotl, Great Mother of the Aztecs, has none of the celestial aloofness of Isis and Mary, but crouches and grimaces in the travail of birth and creation." [5]

Notice the word "travail," which means pain, anguish, suffering. The Christian God decreed that woman shall bring forth life in pain. So here we find a biased, traditionally patriarchal interpretation of the peoples' experience of the birth process. Perhaps the Great Mother's grimace was one of hard work and joy, or maybe...it was a smile! My goodness, what a thought.

Tlazolteotl, Great Mother   **minor female deity**

Drawings by Dusty Bunker

The figure on the right represents the Great Mother who gave birth to the universe from her Yoni. She hardly could be called a "minor" female deity. In fact, it is contradictory to call her a minor deity while stating that the serpent of creative energy is issuing from her vulva. The serpent or snake in all world religions has great power because it represents the creative life energy. This creative energy was not treated kindly by the early Western church, but other cultures look upon it quite differently.

As for calling her a deity (from the male *deus* or god), in *The Changing of the Gods*, Naomi Goldenberg suggests the word "deaty" from *dea* or goddess, the feminine aspect of divinity.

It is important to keep an open mind when examining the

traditional interpretations of the past and what historians believe the relics meant to the people who created them because historians often have a basic belief system into which all things must fit and therefore we get a biased look at history through their eyes.

So, the Vesica Piscis represents divinity, virginity (the independent woman), and her opening (the vulva) through which life emerges into the material world.

The above pictures and descriptions corroborate ancient Mother Goddess religious beliefs that the Great Mother, alone and unaided (the virgin), brought forth life through Her gateway (the vulva or Vesica Piscis) into the world of form.

This is why sacred figures have been portrayed inside the Vesica Piscis. Through the Mother's vulva, the almond-shaped opening, the sacred figures were born. This symbol is the cosmic pattern reflected in the birth process on the physical plane. We are the embodiment of the sacred life energy that emerges from the womb into the world of matter, reflecting the creative life process of nature.

To examine this concept geometrically, let us construct a circle with a diameter of Five, the number of life. You may recall that in our discussion of the number Five, the fifth month of pregnancy is called "the quickening" or the month when life actually enters the fetus in the womb. The circle represents divinity, and in keeping with our images, we shall call it the Mother.

Draw a second circle with a diameter of Five, using any point on the circumference of the first circle as the center of the second. You now have two intersecting circles. The Vesica Piscis is the shaded area in the intersecting circles. It is a basic figure in sacred geometry.

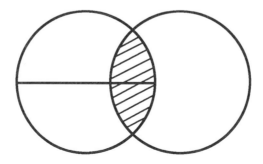

Symbolically, this represents the potential of the Mother (first circle) generating the Child (second circle) through her vulva (the Vesica Piscis): "One generates Two."

"Vesica Piscis" comes from the Latin meaning "bladder of a fish." A bladder is a small sack filled with fluid much like the embryo in the womb is a sack surrounded by fluid. "Vesica" means bladder or blister. When a blister breaks, fluid emerges. Before the birth of a child, the mother's water breaks, indicating that the child is about to emerge.

The Vesica Piscis also was called *ichthus*, which means fish. The Tantric Yoni sometimes was symbolized by a fish. A stylized drawing of a fish, such as that used by early Christians to identify one another ($\Longleftrightarrow$), is similar to the almond shape of the Vesica Piscis or the female vulva.

So, the intersection or the generation of the second circle from the first produces the Vesica Piscis, the opening from the womb of creation through which form eventually emerges.

The sides of the Vesica Piscis represent the opposite poles, the Yin and Yang, the duality that will generate the world of matter. This is the meaning of the pillars guarding the entrance to all holy temples. They can be seen on the Tarot card, Key 2, the Priestess.

Perhaps now it is beginning to become evident why these two simple intersecting circles are considered a basic figure in sacred geometry, and why the simple elegance of geometry is considered sacred. The two circles represent the giver of life and the receiver of life, the opposite polarities necessary to begin the process of creation.

Using the center of the Vesica Piscis, construct a third circle with a diameter of Five. (See the art work on page 37.) You now have another representation of the trinity concept, the Three-in-One, which also has been called the Triple Cord.

The Triple Cord through the center of the Vesica Piscis was one of the best known Hermetic symbols, recognized in various other forms as the serpent circling the tree in the Garden of Eden and as the caduceus, the serpents entwining what we currently know as the medical staff. The staff represents the spine, the ball at the top represents the head, and the snakes represent the life current flowing through the body.

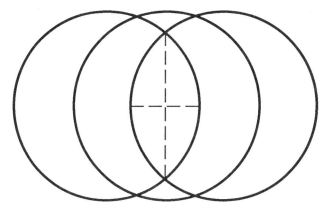

The Triple Cord Through the Vesica Piscis

Another ancient depiction of the Triple Cord is the World Egg surrounded by the Gnostic Serpent. The serpent or snake symbolically represents the creative Life Force that we saw issuing from the minor female deity.

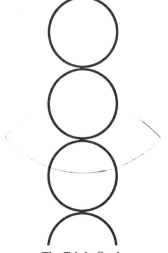

The Triple Cord

The Egyptian hieroglyph for the Triple Cord through the Vesica Piscis was similar to the Hebrew *Cheth* and *Resh*, or *Ch-R*. (The Christians used the monogram X-P to identify this same concept. This can be found in much of their religious art.) The Hebrew word Ch-R is a transposition of the Sanskrit *Rch* meaning "light." Therefore, the Triple Cord emerging from the Vesica Piscis meant the birth of Light from the womb of creation through the vulva.

All things are composed of Light. We as people are solidified Light. Ch-R was personified in Horus, the child in the Egyptian trinity of Isis, Osiris, and Horus, a trinity which was symbolized by the 3-4-5 Pythagorean triangle.

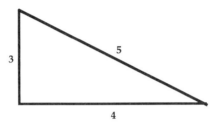

The child is the solidified Light (consciousness or the quickening: 5), in the body (4), brought about by the mix of the trinity (1-2-3, the Triple Cord or the Three-in-One.) "Three generates all things" as was symbolized in the Great Mother's Yoni, the downward pointing triangle of past, present, and future.

The significance is awe-inspiring. These three simple intersecting circles through the Vesica Piscis were initialed "Rch," meaning Light. They represent the birth of Light, or *the birth of every child in the world as the container of the sacred Light*. We are the sacred Light!

Light traditionally has been associated with the creative force. "In religion, legend and symbolism, light is primarily connected with good and with creative power."[6] The general consensus is that darkness preceded the Light. Darkness is "more primitive, more fundamental, and Light penetrates a darkness that was there before it."[7] The Bradaranyaka Upanishad prays, "from darkness lead me to the light...."[8] According to the creation hymn in the Rig Veda, there was only darkness. In Hesiod's *Theogony*, "Out of Void came Darkness and black Night, and out of Night came Light and Day, her children."[9] In the Christian Old Testament, it is written in Genesis that in the beginning there was darkness and the Creator said, "Let there be light."[10] We can see in these creation myths the allegory to coming out of the womb and to the references (in the first chapter) to the cosmic egg of the Great Mother. It was from this womb of darkness that the Light emerged. It was this Light that was the substance that fashioned all creatures.

We also find that the emissaries of the word from each religion were the carriers of the Light--from Ohrmazd in Zoroastrianism to Horus in the Egyptian trinity to Allah in the Koran to Jesus in Christianity.

Light also was associated with illumination and awareness of the divinity within and around. On the road to Damascus, Saint Paul was converted when "a light from heaven flashed about him"[11]; the Mohammedan mystic, Ghazali, was saved from disbelief by a light that came from the Creator; in Indian tradition, the adepts who awaken the kundalini describe it as a magnificent light; the god Vishnu revealed himself in a flash of light; the Eskimo shamans say you cannot become a shaman without experiencing an awareness which they call lightning. [12]

The realization of the profound meaning of these ancient symbols from a variety of religious backgrounds discussed previously hit me recently after studying these manuscripts for years. Collected bits of data suddenly dovetailed in my mind. It was part of the process that produced this book. I was so moved that I wrote the following haiku.

> Form, cast out of Time,
> is home for the sacred Light.
> Kneel. A Child is born.

When our Creator said, "Let there be Light," She was creating life through the child (Rch, the Light) as it emerged through the vulva, the Vesica Piscis, into the world of form. Spirit (the Three-in-One) generated matter (the Four) which became animated (Five) by the Light, the Life Force. The quickening took place. Nature was born from and in Light.

We have been discussing the Three-Four-Five generational series of numbers. Spirit or the Three-in-One generates matter or Four, which generates the solidified Light of Five.

It was said that Pythagoras considered Three the first real number. It is the first number that produces a visible object--the triangle--and philosophically it is synonymous with the One. Three generates all things.

The expression that things happen in threes not only indicates a quantitative assessment of events but also signifies a deeper philosophical meaning: the number Three generates all things. Things happen *in* the number Three. Be aware that through our vocabulary we express truths that we know innately if not consciously.

Since our three circles also can be symbolized by the triangle, and Three-Four-Five is the generational series that produces nature or life as solidified Light, let us construct the classic 3-4-5 Pythagorean triangle in the center of the middle circle.

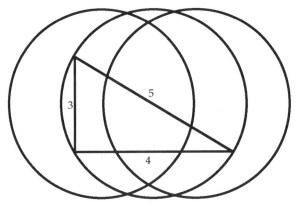

We use the right triangle of Pythagorean fame here rather than an equilateral, isosceles, or scalene triangles because it represents the progressional effects of Three-Four-Five and it also produces the sacred Egyptian bowls that we will discuss shortly. In addition, this figure symbolizes the principle of crossing mentioned on Chapter 1. "This crossing was...a symbol for the process by which things enter into corporeal existence. All birth into nature requires a crossing of opposites."[13] In other words, life is the product of the crossing of opposites, the generation or multiplication (X) from the One.

When examining a right angle such as we find in this right triangle, notice that the horizontal and vertical lines cross at a 90-degree angle. Knowing that sacred geometry lends significance to every line and combination thereof, let's look at the meaning of the horizontal and vertical lines, and their crossing.

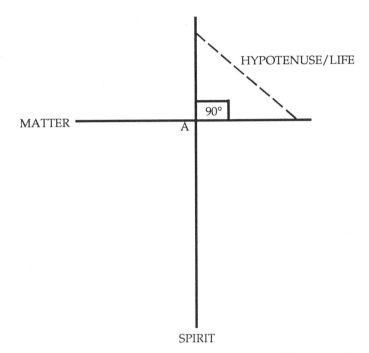

To the ancients the vertical line represented Spirit as it reached for the heights. The horizontal line was a symbol for the world of matter along with the square and its extension, the cube. When the vertical and horizontal lines cross at a 90-degree angle, we have perfect symmetry, the crossing and meeting of Spirit and matter, or time and space, and another symbol for the Earth, the cross.

Where the two lines intersect (point A) is the point of consciousness or the point where the merging of matter from Spirit results in life, symbolized by the hypotenuse, the slanted line of the right triangle.

Two lines intersecting at 90-degree angles can be seen on a graph. It is the diagonal line connecting these junctions that give points of information or awareness about the subject of the graph. (See graph on the following page.)

The four seasons of the year, symbolically a cross, are the equinoxes and solstices that mark the beginning of the new and the end of the old season. They are the result of the play of light from the

Sun over the equator. These are the points of reference in our calendars that provide information about the kind of weather we should expect in our region, the cycles of planting, and even the phases of sales in the marketplace.

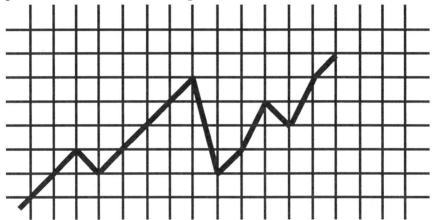

In astrology the angles of the chart symbolically represent the cross and are called the sensitive angles because transits to these points usually are very noticeable, giving us vital information about that part of our lives. In most house systems the angles of an individual's chart are the same, whereas the intermediate house cusps can vary a number of degrees. These angles have a permanence and stability about them, like the square.

In my experience, the square aspects in astrology, planets that are technically in 90-degree orbs to one another, are extremely energized portions of the chart because they create stress points that let you know in no uncertain terms that you are alive. They are points that have to be recognized and dealt with or they continue to unsettle your life. There is a need to find the balance between Spirit and matter or to recognize the Spirit *in* matter. Once handled, the squares provide a great impetus toward accomplishment and a great source of satisfaction.

Therefore, the right angle indicates a point of consciousness in the physical world, which is why it is used in this construction.

The Pythagorean Theorem states that the square of the hypotenuse (the slanted line on the illustration) of a right triangle is equal to the sum of the squares of the other two sides. If we square the hypotenuse of 5 we arrive at 25. If we square the other two sides (3 squared is 9, and 4 squared is 16) and add them (9 + 16) we also arrive at 25. So, 3 squared plus 4 squared equals 5 squared. This formula is a mathematical truth and is used to determine the length of the third side of a triangle when only the values of the other two sides are known.

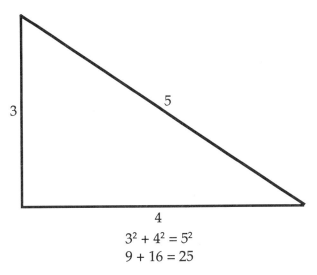

$$3^2 + 4^2 = 5^2$$
$$9 + 16 = 25$$

However, as we know, the ancients viewed numbers differently than we do, seeing them as the ultimate symbolic reduction of philosophical thought. This Pythagorean Theorem has a metaphysical message as well: the sum of the squares (the full potential) of the Three, the vertical line (the creative Spiritual energy), and the Four, the horizontal line (matter) yields Five, the hypotenuse (life or solidified Light).

Just as in a graph where the diagonal line gives living, changing information about the subject of the graph, the diagonal line or the hypotenuse of a right triangle, the Divine Triangle, represents the living and changing essence of life.

Of course, as we mentioned earlier, these initiated ones did not view this formula as addition as the word "sum" implies, but rather as the emergence of each number from its subsequent number.

Hence, the Pythagorean Theorem is useful in practical terms, in the physical world, through numbers as well as in the philosophical sense, in the metaphysical world, through numbers. The pattern of the cosmos is repeated on all levels.

Keep in mind that it is upon the Vesica Piscis, the One generating the Two, that the construction of the circles and the angles is built. The first "real" or visible number, Three (or the triangle), is the result.

At this point our figure is beginning to look complex. But it now should be clear how we arrived at this point and what the sacred geometry before us means.

Our final step is to complete the Three-Four-Five Divine Triangle by drawing its mirror image to construct a rectangle with the proportions 3 X 4 X 3 X 4. In numerology, doubling or squaring a number or its symbol indicates an empowering of the number.

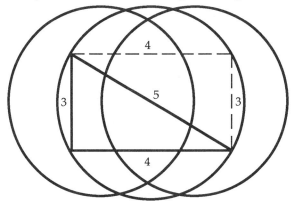

This rectangle (an extended square), symbolizes the birth of the physical, full of Light, from the Vesica Piscis, the opening between the womb of the universe and the world of matter. The rectangle, composed of two Three-Four-Five Divine Triangles, has emerged from the Vesica Piscis.

When contemplating this step in my drawings, one of a series of revelations hit me concerning this book's subject. The importance of the 72-degree quintile and the 108-degree tredecile began to emerge. I had just read the sentences: "The Egyptians, circumscribing the oblong of 3 X 4 within a perfect circle, found the latter divided into segments of 72, 108, 72, and 108 degrees. Such saucer-shaped segments were among their most sacred symbols...." [14]

Here were the most sacred symbols of the Egyptians, the sacred bowls of 72 and 108 degrees, and they had emerged from the Divine Triangle that emerged from the Vesica Piscis! The simple construction of three intersecting circles circumscribing the right triangle in rectangular form was a cosmic message depicting the most creative act possible, that of producing life or solidified Light.

Therefore, the arc of degree that the perfect circle was divided into by this rectangle of 3 X 4 (two divine triangles) was the 72-degree aspect called the quintile and the 108-degree aspect called the tredecile.

These orbs had to be the ultimate creative aspects in nature, and therefore in our personal charts. When the 72-degree shaded areas and the 108-degree shaded areas are brought together, these saucer-shaped segments or sacred bowls return to the Vesica Piscis.

I am using one circle rather than three here in order to clarify the lines. Please keep in mind that it is constructed upon the three circles.

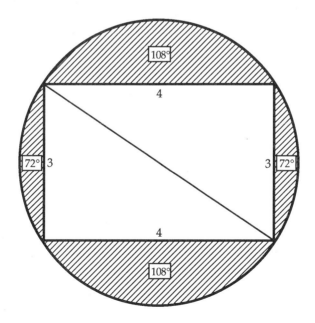

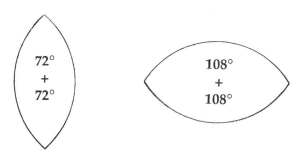

Of course, I had read whatever I could find on the quintile, and subsequently on the tredecile, which is very little. The same information was repeated: these aspects denote talents...mildly beneficial...creative but with little impact... minor aspects... moderately weak...harmonious but carry little weight.

The *Larousse Encyclopedia of Astrology*[15] states that the quintile is regarded as favorable, it denotes talent and power but is a minor aspect that was introduced by Johannes Kepler.

Regarding the quintile, Mark Edmund Jones wrote that it shows talent and how we can link our inner and outer selves, and that this aspect was known only to the initiates of the Chaldean mysteries. It showed the special privilege a person had in relationship to the cosmos. Therefore, through the quintile, you could demand cooperation and spiritual help from the universe. This was creative ability, often latent, through which you could transform your environment through the signs and houses in which the quintile was involved. [16]

Certainly Jones's definition was closer to the truth than the other interpretations that call the quintile a minor and moderately weak aspect with little impact.

Perhaps we should take note of Jones's comment that only the initiates into the Chaldean mysteries knew of the quintile. Is this why even today it is considered a minor aspect?

I have found no lengthy description on the tredecile, only the short phrases mentioned previously--minor easy aspect, carries little weight.

The process of birth and death and rebirth as we have seen from the construction of the Vesica Piscis and Divine Triangle through sacred geometry hardly can be called a minor experience. When I realized what sacred geometry had revealed, I was ecstatic.

Knowing that the quintile or 72-degree orb was named for its division of the circle by Five (from the Latin *quintilis* meaning "fifth"), I divided 108 into the 360 degrees of the circle, and to my utter delight, the answer was 3.33333... ad infinitum.

Three, the first "real" number of the Pythagoreans, the creative Spirit that produces time, the Three that generates all things, was the *symbolic* result of the division of 108 into the circle. Therefore, because of its Three nature and because of reasons explained in Chapter 4, I feel that "tredecile" is an appropriate term for this orb.

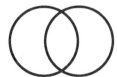

I also feel that the perfect symbol for this aspect is the two intersecting circles that create the Vesica Piscis and subsequently resulted in this aspect. Again, this symbol reflects its companion symbol, the quintile (Q).

The geometric drawings on my desk proved the "creativeness" of the quintile and tredecile. I knew that if indeed these were the ultimate creative aspects in the chart, these numbers of 72, the quintile (the fifth division, 5 on the Divine Triangle representing life) and 108, the tredecile (the symbolic third division of a circle, and 3 on the Divine Triangle representing the creative aspect of time), would have to be repeated throughout nature in the most profound and meaningful of places. We will explore these numbers in the next chapter.

For now, Three is the creative number forever (or as long as the universe is set up the way it is). The 108-degree aspect is the 3.333... ad infinitum, a division of the circle indicating that this aspect is the creativity that goes on forever, living long after the physical body is transformed. It is the relationship of time with the eternal.

In the introduction I mentioned an incident that occurred early in my life. I would like to relate this now because it is tied in with and perhaps was the impetus for this book.

I was five years old. I was sitting at my desk in the first grade class room intently studying my primer, trying to figure out what the strange glyphs on the pages meant. Suddenly, it all came together. I read my first sentence.

See Spot run.

A wave of power washed down over my body. It was real, alive, and palpitating. I physically could feel its presence. What I only can describe as my soul expanded and extended beyond my physical body. In my child's mind, I recognized I had touched something sacred, something that could change my world. At that moment I knew my destiny. I would read and write and fill books with this power that filled my soul so that others would know its transforming ecstasy. I would search the mysteries of the universe so that I would know.

I now know that power was the power of the word. That feeling has never left me.

I have never been able to sufficiently explain this intense transforming experience or my subsequent dedication and immersion in the quest for knowledge until I came upon the tredecile.

Yes, I have Mercury in Scorpio in the Fourth House, which could indicate researching intensely into the roots of being, and the Moon in Sagittarius in the Fifth House, suggesting a love of wisdom. But as a Scorpio I was disappointed that my Mercury was not in aspect to Pluto because I felt the intensity of that association in every fiber of my being. It did not seem enough that Mercury was in Scorpio, which is ruled by Pluto.

The revelation I had while riding home from Conner Pond that fateful morning (see the Introduction) finally fulfilled my desire to be connected with Pluto because I suddenly realized that I have Mercury exactly tredecile Pluto in the 12th House. When I was five years old and learned the power of the word, the progressed sun was transiting my natal Mercury, setting off that aspect. I was finally home!

Chapter 3
The Quintile and Tredecile Explained

Out of the Vesica Piscis (Mother-Child/One-Two) emerged the Three that generates all things.

We have seen how the equilateral triangle, the geometric representation of the Three, symbolizes time: past, present, and future; beginning, middle, end; youth, adulthood, old age. We also have seen how time was personified in Maiden, Mother, Crone; Mother, Father, Child; Brahma, Vishnu, Shiva; Isis, Osiris, Horus and so forth throughout all cultures.

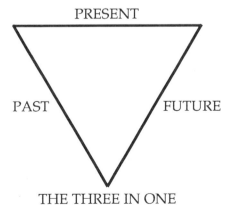

THE THREE IN ONE

In the Three-Four-Five Divine Triangle, the creative process is put into operation.

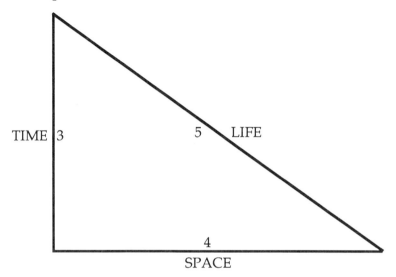

Time (Three) generates or produces space (Four) which in turn produces life or solidified Light (Five). So time births space, which births the container for the Light or solidified Light, the animated physical form. The human experience pattern is the mother and the father giving birth to the Light of the world in the child. This child of Light has been elevated in various cultures around the earth in personalities such as Buddha, Horus, Mohammed, Jesus, and so forth. However, this child of Light represents every child born on this planet, female and male. We are all the children of Light.

In fact, all creatures on earth are solidified Light--the birds, fish, insects, and animals--which is why Pythagoras taught his students that the eating of the flesh of any creature was wrong.

In *Metamorphoses*, Ovid, when describing the teachings of Pythagoras, writes:

> Oh, what a wicked thing it is for flesh
> To be the tomb of flesh, for the body's craving
> To fatten on the body of another,
> For one live creature to continue living

Through one live creature's death. In all the richness
That Earth, the best of mothers, tenders to us,
Does nothing please except to chew and mangle
The flesh of slaughtered animals? The Cyclops
Could do no worse!... [1]

All creatures are solidified Light born through time and the emergence of space, which allows form in the Three-Four-Five triangle. Each people identified this divine process of birth through their own cultural bias, which reflected what they knew and experienced on an everyday level. The process had to have personal meaning. Although the outward details of the birth of Light vary from culture to culture, the crux of the story remains the same. Time produces space produces solidified Light, which is the physical embodiment of the One Light, the One Creative Force. This is the Three-in-One.

The Light also was evident in daily life, for without the movement of the Sun over the equator to produce the seasons, there would be no life on Earth as we know it. Light from the Sun gave us a measure of earthly time, the seasons, and allowed life to flourish.

The movement of light through space also gives us a measure of time. Light travels at 186,000 miles per second, so it is possible to measure the time it takes for light from distant stars to reach our planet. The Light always has been connected with time and life.

I write this during the Christmas season and find that the holiday takes on new meaning for me. Lines from "O Holy Night" run through my mind, over and over. They fill me with an expanding glow, a Light, a reverence for the divine creative process. Understanding this process through sacred geometry had opened a doorway into a land of reverence that the personal story of Mary, Joseph, and Jesus had not done. Now I can look upon both representations of the creative process with a feeling of connection and a new liberated awareness. I feel akin to Euclid who "alone has looked on beauty bare." [2]

The Three-Four-Five Divine Triangle divides the circle into arcs of 72, 108, 72, 108 as we have seen. To further understand what these aspects mean in astrological charts, we should examine them symbolically. As I said earlier, these numbers should have terrestrial and cosmic significance if they are meaningful.

The rectangle produced by the Vesica Piscis and the Divine Triangle represents the entrance into the physical world. It is through this doorway that we are born and return to be reborn again.

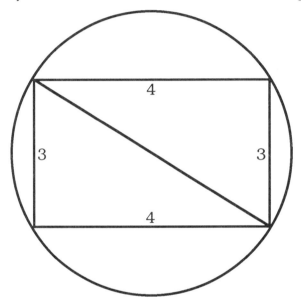

The double Three-Four-Five Divine Triangle or the 3 X 4 X 3 X 4 rectangle emerging from the Vesica Piscis is the symbol of eternal rebirth through the womb of creation. It contains two Three-Four-Five triangles emphasizing the duality of the Light, one expression encased in the physical, the other outside the physical, suggesting the cycle of birth into this world (or death from another world) and death from this world (or birth into another world). It also suggests the continual cycling of this process. This doctrine of reincarnation or metamorphosis was the final secret taught at ancient mystery schools.

By examining gematria, where a glyph can indicate both a letter as well as a number, we discover fascinating philosophical and metaphysical correlations hidden behind the word and the number.

The Old Testament of the Christian Bible was written in Aramaic, the language of Jesus. The New Testament is a Greek book. Although it is believed that the oral traditions of Jesus' life and deeds were in Aramaic, the language of Palestine, it was soon after that these traditions were translated into Greek, the language of the civilized Mediterranean world at that time. Therefore, the New Testament is in Greek. So we need to examine both Hebrew and Greek gematria in order to understand these people's philosophical reduction of thought through numbers.

Each glyph of the Hebrew and Greek alphabets has a number value so that words and numbers represent more than what they appear to the uninitiated. [3]

In Revelations, the writer speaks of the 144,000 saved, or the number of spiritual souls who will be saved at the end of the world. The word that was translated as "world" also could be read as "Age" so that this passage could be interpreted as the number of souls who will be saved at the end of the "Age," which can refer to the Precession of the Equinoxes, certainly a more likely translation.

Keep in mind that the length of an Age is approximately 2,160 years, a number that figures importantly in our discussion. Also remember that the use of zeros after digits often was an emphasis or empowering of the numbers involved. The doubling of numbers represented the energy in process as it magnified.

If we take the two arcs of 72 degrees in our circle that is intersected by the two Divine Triangles and merge them in the center, we have created a symbolic Vesica Piscis, the doorway to the womb of creation.

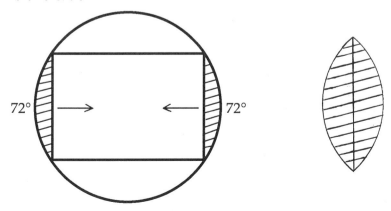

This Vesica Piscis measures 144 degrees of arc--the number of the saved in Revelations--those who will be saved through rebirth. The Vesica Piscis is the entrance to the womb of creation; this smaller Vesica Piscis measures 144 degrees of arc. It is through this dual portal that we are born into each single lifetime, 72 degrees (the quintile), and return, 72 degrees, to be born again. The two sides (72 and 72) designate the eternal cycle (144) of rebirth through the womb of creation.

Therefore, the 144,000 saved in the Bible are all of us! We all are saved through the sacred process of birth, death, and rebirth through the womb of creation, the Vesica Piscis, because we are temporary manifestations of Light from the One Light which eternally solidifies, changes form, and solidifies once again.

One-hundred and forty-four is also a multiple of 12 (12 X 12) and, in this sense, designates the empowering of the twelvefold pattern of the zodiac in which we unfold each lifetime.

In addition, when we add the values of Three-Four-Five found on the Divine Triangle, the geometric blueprint of life, we arrive at 12 (3 + 4 + 5 = 12). This again signifies that the pattern of each individual life is twelvefold (like the steps through the zodiacal wheel).

It would seem that the 72-degree aspect or the quintile relates to one single lifetime. Does this symbolically carry through other numbers?

It is said that the average pulse in the human being is 72 beats per minute, during which time four liters of blood are pumped through the heart. One minute is symbolic of a lifetime of minutes.

The period of 72 years corresponds to one "great day" in the "Great Year" of the 25,960 years of the Precession of the Equinoxes. It takes 72 years for the Earth's pole to move through one degree of the 360-degree circle it describes in the heavens because of the Earth's wobble--this movement is known as the Precession of the Equinoxes.

We could look upon the "great day" as the length of time, 72 years or one lifetime, that it takes to unfold our latent talents, the 72-degree quintile.

The "great day" is 72 years, and the average pulse is 72 beats per minute, all symbolic of one complete cycle or one lifetime. Seventy-two degrees is the quintile. In astrological progressions we take one day to symbolize one year; in one "great day" of 72 years we can symbolize one lifetime.

We can now see how the quintile, the "talent,"[4] or more appropriately, the capabilities we have brought in from the past, should be used as a source of further development in this lifetime.

The 72-degree aspect, the quintile, as a fifth division of the circle, represents life (the value 5 on the hypotenuse of the Divine Triangle, which is solidified Light or this one life that we presently live).

The quintile is the fifth harmonic, and as the fifth, it symbolically activates Light as shown on the Three-Four-Five Divine Triangle. The quintile is indeed a creative aspect that indicates latent talents that can unfold during this lifetime. It is the Light we carry within that can be activated or manifested during our life.

The inevitable conclusion is that the 72-degree aspect, as half of the 144, represents forces or talents at work in this half of our experience while we are in the physical manifestation of Light, while we are in the body. It is something to be used and developed now because it represents this one life.

Let's examine the tredecile, ⬭ , the 108-degree aspect. The larger arcs of the intersected circle are 108 degrees each.

Earlier we saw the Hermetic symbol of the Triple Cord emerging through the Vesica Piscis. The name for this symbol is Ch-R, a transposition of the Sanskrit Rch, meaning Light. In the New Testament, which was written in Greek, Jesus was called the Son of Light, the Light of the world, who emerged from his mother, Mary, or the Vesica Piscis.

In the Greek alphabet the values of the letters Ch and R are 8 and 100--which add to 108 or the tredecile! Therefore, Jesus as the child, and Horus as the child, and all other children of the holy trinity, and all children of the world, were and are the Light of the world. The deeds of the holy children of the trinities lived on long after their physical bodies were gone. They left profound messages of truth for the world to study and ponder and to find comfort and faith in. They left their Light for the world for ages.

These Light children grew into adults who left a lasting story for each culture. They are a metaphor for all the children born into this world as solidified Light--including you and me. And we, as the Light children, add to 108 or the tredecile.

When brought to the center of the diagram, the two arcs of 108 degrees form a Vesica Piscis of 216 degrees. With the addition of a zero, this Vesica Piscis becomes 2,160, or the number of years we traditionally deem an Age in the Precession of the Equinoxes! (Strangely, the Moon's diameter is estimated at 2,160 miles, and it is the Moon's gravitational pull on the Earth that is involved in the Precession of the Equinoxes.)

Each Age in the Precession of the Equinoxes has a specific message or symbolic pattern that is imprinted on the universe for the duration of that Age. This is reflected in the religious rituals that spring up around the definition of the Age.

For instance, from about 4,000 B.C. to 2,000 B.C., the Age of Taurus, worship centered around the Bull and its counterpart, the Eagle, Phoenix, or Falcon (Scorpio).

From 2,000 B.C. to 0 A.D., the Age of Aries reigned where lambs were sacrificed in fire (Aries is a fire sign) and Moses came down off the mountain with the two tablets declaring the laws (Libra, the opposite sign of Aries). He then admonished the people to stop worshipping the golden calf (the Age of Taurus was over).

From roughly 0 to 2,000 A.D., we have been in the Age of Pisces, which baptizes in water (Pisces is a water sign). The early Christians used the sign of the fish (Pisces) to identify one to another when it was dangerous to openly declare one's faith. The opposite sign, Virgo, rules the grain and grapes or bread and wine, which is used in the sacramental rituals. This sign also rules the symbology of the Virgin Mother in Christianity.

History proves that each Age imprinted its particular wisdom on the collective subconscious of the planet as the Earth's pole moved through that part of the Precession of the Equinoxes.

My point is that the *fullest* expression of the 108- degree tredecile or the 216-degree Vesica Piscis (108 + 108) is the Light we leave for the Age we live in. In the case of those of us living now, this aspect indicates the new Light we shine to help with the transition into the Age of Aquarius. What a nice thought!

Where else can we find the 108 in metaphysical terms? My husband and I are movie fans. Fanatics, I must admit. We recently viewed the movie *Bull Durham*, about a woman involved with baseball players. I never expected to obtain a piece of information for this book from that film, but indeed it happened. In the beginning of the film, the voice of leading actress Susan Sarandon is heard in the background as the camera pans a room. She is speaking of her search for meaning in life and she happens to mention that there are 108 beads in a rosary. You can imagine that my ears perked up when I heard that. I went to the library the following morning.

The word "rosary" comes from the Latin *rosarium*, meaning "rose garden." Rosaries in all forms are a string of beads or knots used in prayer and devotions. They can be found in widespread use in many religions and may have originated in Hindu India.

The Jain rosaries have 108 beads or multiples of this number. The Sikhs use rosaries of 108 knots or iron beads. In Mahayanna Buddhism, the prayer rope usually has 108 beads. The rosary commonly used in the Roman Catholic Church has 50 small beads separated by four large beads. The first multiple of 54 is 108.

The prayer beads are a way of elevating the soul, keeping oneself centered in a busy world, and maintaining a connection with the teachings of one's religion. By chanting a mantra or prayer over and over while touching each bead, one moves into a trancelike or meditative state, much like the state produced by the rhythmic drumbeats in Indian or African rituals. This meditative state allows one to experience a reality above or beyond the present worldly condition. It reinforces the knowledge that there are two worlds of reality, one that we can see and touch and smell, and another that cannot be seen but is felt. It allows the balancing of heart and mind, when the lion (Leo-heart) lies down with the lamb (Aries-head). Our religion should bring about this meeting if our lives are to be full and productive.

The rosary with its 108 beads symbolically connects us to the cosmic message of the religion we practice. This religion is the result of the Age of 2,160 (a multiple of 108, the tredecile) in which we live. The rosary is a connection to the imprinted pattern of the present Age in the Precession of the Equinoxes.

I also happened to come across an article in *Time* magazine about the date 8-8-88.

> For the Japanese, the character that represents the nu-
> meral (Eight), two vertical lines widening toward the bottom
> indicates suehirogari, or increasing prosperity....To observe
> the once-in-a century day, nearly 1,000 Japanese climbers
> gathered at the top of Fuji in the early-morning hours of the
> 8th. They erected a cairn at the crest with 216 stones collected
> from mountains whose names include the word fuji.... [5]

One can only imagine why they chose 216 stones.

Also, we find the 108 symbolically nestled in the human physi-
ology. The average rhythm of the heart is eighteen breaths a minute
during which four liters of blood are pumped. In one hour we take
1080 breaths (18 X 60). In one day we breathe 25,920 times (1080 X 24).
The 1080 breaths per hour relates to the tredecile, symbolically
addressing the longer period of time, or one Age (2160 years) in the
Precession of the Equinoxes. (You may recall that by bringing the
two arcs of 108 degrees together in our diagram we form a Vesica
Piscis of 216 degrees.) This could be called the "Great Month."

The 25,920 breaths per day approximates the time in years it
takes for the sun at the spring equinox to make one complete
revolution of the zodiac back to its original point at the spring
equinox, or the completion of the Precession of the Equinoxes, which
is called the "Great Year."

So, the 108-degree aspect, as the 3.333... symbolic division of the
circle, symbolizes the creativity that lives on after us, for our Age. It
is a composite of hard work and effort and thought and creative development in this one lifetime, which can be enhanced by the
quintiles we already have, although the quintiles are not necessary
for the tredecile to work. The tredecile aspect of 108 degrees is what
history will say about us when we trade in this physical body. It is
the part of us that lives on forever...it is our holy work whether it be
in a garden or on the Moon...it is the Light we leave for others.

To review these two aspects: the 72-degree quintile, also expressed by the 144-degree arc created by the two Divine Triangles

built off the smaller Vesica Piscis, represents a smaller, in terms of time, expression of our creativity.

We have seen that the 72 is symbolically related to one lifetime through our discussion of the 72 heartbeats per minute and the 72 years it takes for the pole to move through one degree of the circle of the Precession of the Equinoxes, called the Great Day.

We find that the 144 (a multiple of 72) is an amplification of the 12 zodiacal signs (12 X 12), a pattern or process of unfolding that is experienced each lifetime (each of the 12 signs rules an area of life and therefore each sign is expressed in a lifetime).

The 144,000 saved who are spoken of inRevelations in the Christian Bible are in reality each one of us who are saved by the eternal birth and rebirth through the Vesica Piscis, the Great Mother's genital area, created by the two 72-degree arcs or 144 degrees! This is the promise of reincarnation, recycling, rebirth through the most creative act of all: giving birth.

The quintile aspect is the most creative tool we can use during this life to enhance all our qualities and potentials.

The 108-degree tredecile, also expressed by the 216-degree arc created by the two Divine Triangles built off the larger Vesica Piscis, represents a larger (in terms of time) expression of our creativity.

We found that the transposition of the word for Light from the Sanskrit comes down to us through Greek gematria in the New Testament of the Christian Bible (Christianity is the embodiment of the Age of Pisces) as Ch-R, or 108. Ch-R, as the child of the trinity (the Three that generates all things) is the child of Light personified in Horus, Buddha, Mohammed, Jesus, and others. Jesus was the representative of the Age of Pisces. He was the Light of this Age. He said anything he could do we could do and more. His message was that he symbolized what we all are: children of Light. He did what we all can do: honor that Light as the Creative Force of the universe.

One hundred and eight also can be multiplied to make 2160, the length of an Age in the Precession of the Equinoxes that we could call the Great Month. It also is the number of beads commonly found around the world in rosaries, prayer beads that are used to enter that meditative state that connects us to the greater message of our Age.

Therefore, the 108-degree tredecile indicates the Light you carry that can be expressed in this lifetime and will surely live beyond your physical body as a measure of who you were and what you did. It is the Light of love and awareness that you leave for the advancement of your Age. The tredecile is your contribution to the creative pool of the universe. It is your ultimate creative potential that will become a living force in your Precessional Age.

Chapter 4
Thirty-six, the Decile: The Oath of Secrecy

It has been written that the Pythagoreans swore their oaths of secrecy on the number 36. I have wondered about this for some time, knowing that numbers represent philosophical ideas as well as celestial and terrestrial measurements. Therefore, the number 36 had to incorporate both the philosophical and the corporeal in order to have brought about its position of honor among the Pythagoreans.

Of course, 36 is one-tenth of a circle of 360 degrees, hence its name "decile." The Ten was one of the honored numbers of the Pythagoreans expressed in the diagram called the Tetraktys.

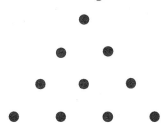

It would seem there was much behind the 36 in order for this number to stand as the binding commitment to the secrets of an ancient, revered order. Since my birth number and house number are 36, I was even more intrigued. Is it a coincidence that I am a numerologist and have a large library on numerology, sacred geometry, philosophy, astrology, and other related subjects?

German astrologer, astronomer, and mathematician Johannes Kepler (1571-1630) was the first to formulate a general theory of aspects and he is credited with the discovery of the decile series. The decile and its multiples are shown in the table below along with their glyphs.

36 X 1 = 36   semi-quintile or decile ⊥

36 X 2 = 72   quintile Q

36 X 3 = 108   tredecile or trecile or sesquiquintile ‡
                   (I propose the glyph ⓪ for the tredecile)

36 X 4 = 144   biquintile ⊥

36 X 5 = 180   the opposition O-O

Continuing the series of multiplication, we have:

36 X 6 = 216   Clockwise this leaves 144 degrees in the circle
                   (the biquintile).

36 X 7 = 252   Clockwise this leaves 108 degrees in the circle
                   (the tredecile)

36 X 8 = 288   Clockwise this leaves 72 degrees in the circle
                   (the quintile)

36 X 9 = 324   Clockwise this leaves 36 degrees in the circle
                   (the semi-quintile)

36 X 10 = 360 the circle

In numerology, 36 can be written as 36/9 because 3 + 6 = 9. Visually we are reminded of three triangles

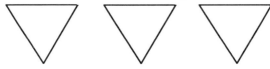

or, in the number of lines, 3 - 6 - 9. This triple suggestion is symbolic of the Triple Cord or the creative Life Force that can be found in many ancient secret teachings in a variety of representations.

In Christianity the Triple Cord is the serpent as the life current circling the tree in the Garden of Eden. In the healing arts, it is the caduceus or the medical staff where the serpents or the Life Force encircle the staff or the spine. The sphere at the top is the head; the wings are the heightened consciousness of which wo/man is capable.

In ancient Hindu teachings, the extent of human life was said to be 108 years (36 X 3, or the life current circling the staff three-plus times). Two times 108 is 216, the philosophical number of rebirth or reincarnation in their teachings (with the addition of a zero, it is the length of an Age). The Pythagoreans also called 216 the number of metempsychosis or reincarnation. They used the following cabalistic diagram to embody this idea.

$$
\begin{array}{ll}
4 \quad 5 = 9 \\
6 \quad 3 = 9 \\
2 \quad 7 = 9 \\
8 \quad 1 = 9 \\
\hline
\cdot 216 \cdot \quad 36
\end{array}
$$

Therefore, the life current, the Creative Force in the universe, was represented by 36 and its multiples. 36 was the Sun, the Solar Logos, whose serpentine movement over the equator ensured that life would flourish. This was the creative life current embodied in the Sun and its movement.

Notice that the dotted lines in the above diagram form the Triple Cord mentioned in Chapter 2. This is the same Triple Cord that the snake forms around the apple tree in the Garden of Eden, and the two snakes form around the caduceus.

To the Pythagoreans, 36 was the numerical indicator of the sacred Life Force and the material world in which that Life Force manifested itself. Further substantiation is possible through understanding the order of the numbers that reveal a pattern of development--not only philosophically but also psychologically and physically.

All creation evolves through the number pattern One through Nine. The Seven "days" of creation spoken of in the Christian Bible are seven steps in a process that would lead to physical manifestation or the world of form. No form was created in the first seven days or steps. The pattern was formed.

The Creator rested on the seventh day because Seven is the number of rest, when the energies of the first six cycles are ingested, internalized, and understood. Seven is the thought process, the planning stage where the pattern is put together, prior to tangible results.

Therefore the physical world was created on the eighth "day." It is under the Eight that the world of form, as the direct and equal result of the preparation under stages One through Seven, finally manifests. It is under the Nine that all form dissolves and returns to be recycled or born anew under the One.

Therefore, Eight, geometrically represented by the cube--the salt of the earth (salt crystallizes in cube form)--is the number of the tangible results of the Divine Triangle processes.

We shall see shortly why this Eight is important in this discussion. First, *one* of the names of the Creator is Jod-Heh-Vau-Heh, whose number value adds to an Eight. ($10 + 5 + 6 + 5 = 26; 2 + 6 = 8$; written as 26/8.) Jod-Heh-Vau-Heh or Jehovah represents the aspect of the Creator that brings tangible results. (Remember that the Creator had many names, depending on what aspect was functioning at the time. Many of these names can be resolved into celestial and terrestrial measurements.) This sacred name is the number code for the diagram called the Sacred Trapezoid. (See the diagram on page 65.)

The name Jod-Heh-Vau-Heh and its diagram represent the Earth's relationship to the Sun, without which there would be no Life on this planet as we know it. If the Earth's pole were vertical to the ecliptic (the path it travels around the Sun), the Sun's light always would shine over the equator and we would have no seasons. As a result, we would have no life that is now familiar to us.

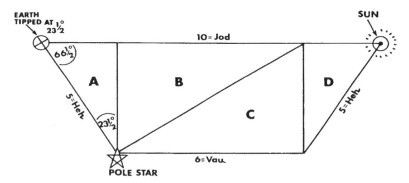

The four-part name of Jod-Heh-Vau-Heh also symbolizes the four seasons that it creates through the relationship between the Earth and the Sun. As shown above, we find the number Eight hidden in the name of Jehovah.

The extension of Eight, or $1 + 2 + 3 + 4 + 5 + 6 + 7 + 8$ is 36, can be written as $1 \rightarrow 8 = 36$. The extension of a number is the sum of all the energies required to arrive at that result. Hence, philosophically and corporeally, 36 represents the process that caused the manifestation of life as the result of the Sun's light playing over the earth. Therefore 36 was called the number of the Sun or the Solar Logos or Solar Word.

The Solar Logos, the 36, also can be seen on the Divine Triangle. (See the figure on page 66.)

Take the values of the sides of the triangle--Three, Four, Five--and multiply them by Three, the triangle, the creative Life Force. The subsequent sums of 9, 12, and 15 add to 36.

Remember our earlier discussion about the Three as the Great Mother's Yoni? Three is the creative number indicating time: past, present, and future. Life springs from the Three or the Three-in-One. The all-seeing eye of Horus from Egyptian lore expresses this concept. It is a stylized drawing of the Divine Triangle sometimes depicted within a circle or a triangle. (See drawing on page 60.)

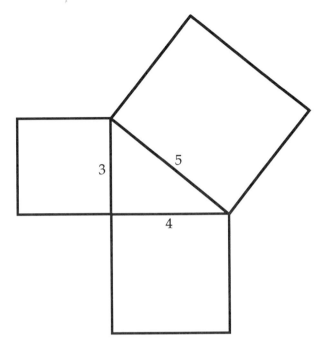

3 AS THE ▽: CREATIVE LIFE FORCE

$$3 \times SIDE\ 3 =\ 9$$
$$3 \times SIDE\ 4 = 12$$
$$3 \times SIDE\ 5 = \underline{15}$$
$$36$$

The All-Seeing Eye

Thirty-six was called the Solar Logos because Logos (meaning "word") creates a vibration just as the spoken word sends vibrations into the air waves. This movement ultimately creates. Creation is the result of a moving vibration, which is why there is such an emphasis in the Bible on the word of the Creator. Therefore, the Solar Logos is the creative force of the Sun.

The Pythagoreans swore their oaths on the number 36, the decile, the Solar Logos, or the Sun. The 36 represents the extension of Eight, the solidification of the orderly and evolving pattern of life, and the Divine Triangle, the marriage of time (Three) and space (Four) that created nature or life (Five). This honoring of 36 was a devotion to and recognition of the connection between time and eternity. It was their attempt to answer those great and eternal questions: Who am I? Where did I come from? Where am I going? and What is my place in the cosmic scheme of things? These geometric/numerological/astrological messages convinced them that there was a Divine Presence that set up our beautifully ordered universe. The 36 was their connection to eternity.

The 36 is the root of the decile aspect and its multiples because Ten (decile) divided into the circle (360 degrees) yields 36. The 72-degree quintile (36 X 2) and the 108-degree tredecile (36 X 3) are the results of the Divine Triangle constructed within the circles of the Vesica Piscis, the Great Mother's opening.

With the magnitude and awesome beauty of this ancient body of philosophic and celestial/terrestrial proof honoring the sacred Life force through the quintile and tredecile, surely we cannot consider these aspects minor.

Footnotes

Introduction

[1] Steven's letter uses the term "tritile" which I had called this 108-degree aspect early in my research. I have since realized that tredecile is the better term for reasons which are explained in the text.
[2] From "Here On In," reprinted in *Geocosmic News*, vol. 12, no. 1, fall 1987.

In the Beginning

[1] Lao-tzu, *Tao Te Ching* [China, about 600 B.C.] from Carl Sagan, *Cosmos*. New York: Random House, 1980, p. 245.
[2] J.C. Cooper, *An Illustrated Encyclopedia of Traditional Symbols*. London: Thames and Hudson, 1978, p. 60.
[3] Barbara Walker, *Woman's Encyclopedia of Myths and Secrets*. New York: Harper and Row, Publishers Inc., 1983, pp.1097-1098.
[4] *Ibid..*, p. 349.
[5] Cooper, *Encyclopedia*, p. 113.
[6] Carl Sagan, *Cosmos*. New York: Random House, 1980, p. 246.
[7] Isaac Asimov, *The Universe*. New York: Walker and Company, 1908, pp. 210-211. From Belgian astronomer Georges Edward Lemaitre, 1927, my word in brackets.
Author's note: Only females produce eggs.
[8] Parthenogenetically: development of an egg without fertilization.
[9] Judy Chicago, *The Dinner Party*. New York: Doubleday/Anchor Books, 1979, pp. 8-20.

Chapter 1

[1] Lao-tzu, *Tao Te Ching*, from Carl Sagan, *Cosmos*. New York: Random House, 1980, p. 245.
[2] Schwaller de Lubicz, R.A., *The Temple in Man*. New York: Inner Traditions International, 1977. Translated by Robert and Deborah

Lawlor, translator's foreword, p. 10.

[3] Schwaller, *Temple*, p. 10.

[4] Isaac Azimov, *The Universe*. New York: Walker and Company, 1980, pp. 210-211.

[5] Sagan, *Cosmos*, p. 246.

[6] Dusty Bunker, *Numerology, Astrology and Dreams*. West Chester, Pa.: Whitford Press/Schiffer Publishing, Ltd., 1988, pp. 95-96.

[7] *Random House Dictionary of the English Language*. New York: Random House, 1969.

[8] *Ibid.*

[9] *Encyclopedia Americana*, vol. 18. New York: Americana Corporation, 1966.

[10] *Ibid.*, p. 718.

Chapter 2

[1] Paul Higgins, *Hermetic Masonry*. New York: Pyramid Publishing Company, 1916; Ferndale, Michigan: Trismegistus Press, 1980, p. 91.

[2] J.C. Cooper, *An Illustrated Encyclopedia of Traditional Symbols*. London: Thames and Hudson, 1978, p.185.

[3] *Ibid.*, pp. 103-104.

[4] *Random House Dictionary of the English Language*. New York: Random House, 1969.

[5] Cooper, *Illustrated Encyclopedia*, p. 149.

[6] Richard Cavendish, *Man, Myth, and Magic*. New York: Marshall, Cavendish, 1985, pp. 1622-1630.

[7] *Ibid.*

[8] *Ibid.*

[9] *Ibid.*

[10] *Ibid.*

[11] *Ibid.*

[12] *Ibid.*

[13] Schwaller de Lubicz, R.A.,*The Temple in Man*. New York: Inner Traditions International, 1977. Translated by Robert and Deborah Lawlor, translator's foreword, p. 10.

[14] Higgins, *Hermetic Masonry*, pp. 88-89.

[15] *Larousse Encyclopedia of Astrology*. New York: New American

Library, 1982, p. 237.
[16] From the *Digested Astrologer*, Search, Box 162, North Gate Station, Seattle, Washington 98125.

Chapter 3

[1] Ovid, *Metamorphoses*, translated by Rolfe Humphries, Blooming-ton, Illinois: Indiana University Press, 1955, p. 368.

[2] Edna St. Vincent Millay, "Euclid Alone Has Looked On Beauty Bare," 1923, line 11.

[3] An interesting aside. Pythagoras spoke of three groups of people: the novitiate--those who don't know and don't know that they don't know; the initiate--those who don't know and know that they don't know; and the illuminati--those who know and know that they know. Sometimes the first group thinks they are the third.

[4] My definition of talent is an ability that we have worked on and developed so well in the past, perhaps past lifetimes, that we can do it much better than most. This reminds me of the story of a man who approached a great composer and performer after a symphony and gushed about how lucky the composer was to be so talented. The composer replied, "Sir, if you practiced ten hours a day for forty years, you would be just as talented as I."

Part II: A [eated ...ecile ,.nition

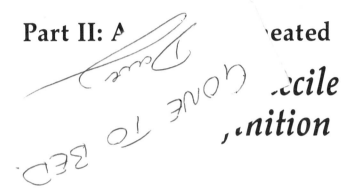

In Indian astrology a primary method of analyzing aspects is through house association. For example, the conjunction is related to the First House, the sextile has a Third- and EleventhHouse reference, the square a Fourth and Tenth House connection, and so forth. The theory is that by using the general meanings of the houses involved in the aspect, one is able to better understand the aspect in question. I find this method helpful when teaching astrology as long as it is not taken to extremes.

Let's look at the quintile and tredecile using this method. When one point of the quintile, a 72-degree aspect, is placed on the First House cusp, which is your view of reality and always is implied in your understanding, the other point falls into the Third House going in a counterclockwise direction and in the Tenth House when moving in a clockwise fashion. Therefore, if we take the general meanings of the Third and Tenth Houses into consideration, we get the idea behind the quintile.

The Third House is communication in the local area as opposed to Ninth House communication which involves contact with foreigners, distant places, and the universe. The Third House is the concrete mind where one's private thoughts and mental concentration are focussed on gathering information from personal experience that comes from contact with the local environment. The Third House is your personal thought process that is accessible and communicable.

The Tenth House is the manifestation and public recognition of personal efforts. It is the place of those authority figures that have gained praise and/or credit for some achievement. This is the House of reputation--either notoriety or fame.

By combining these two house meanings, the quintile emerges as those personal ideas that gain public recognition. It is the experience taken in that is formulated through ideas that then are made accessible to the public. So the quintile represents the public recognition of personal thought.

The quintile is called a minor aspect, easy and slightly favorable. It was said to be hidden talent. Mark Edmund Jones said that it shows talent and how we can link our inner and outer selves, that it was known only to initiates of the Chaldean mysteries, and that it is creative ability, often latent, with which we can transform the environment.

It may have been called a hidden talent because not everyone is willing to put in the energy required to transform ideas into concrete reality. So the ideas remain inside, hidden, unused. We can link our inner and outer selves through this aspect by making our ideas work in the physical world, by turning them into something usable and practical in the sense that we benefit from them and subsequently others will benefit as well because of the person our thought processes make us.

The quintile is creative because it comes from our personal thoughts and experiences that are unique to us. By using this aspect properly, we indeed can transform the environment because our mind creates our reality. If we manifest our ideas, our reality changes in tangible ways.

For example, I have dreamed of my own office space in my home for years, a nook in the corner of the house that would be totally mine. I have worked in the kitchen on an ironing board between the high chairs and the kitchen table, and in the living room on a clipboard when the kitchen overfloweth, and sometimes in my bed under a mini-light with stacks of book threatening to collapse on the floor beside me. The office I wanted would be the culmination of my dream that I was indeed a writer and deserving of my own working space. That dream has been a thought for the past ten years. Last spring, I made a decision that I would turn a room off the side of the house into my place now that it was no longer needed for bedroom space. I hired a carpenter/friend and the two of us spent three months working on this room a few hours a day. I designed and decorated the room just the way I wanted it with no reference to anyone else's needs. It had to be my room. (At 51 years of age, and after raising four children, I gave myself permission to indulge my wants.) The room is quite beautiful with extras that weren't technically necessary but emotionally required. (Of course, Pluto transiting my Sun at 13 degrees Scorpio in the Fourth House helped.)

This all came about during a series of national exposures of my work or my thought processes. A few months before the construction, I was hired by Time-Life Books as a consultant on their new series, *Mysteries of the Unknown*. That book came out in the spring while my office was being built. Also, in May I was mentioned in an article in *New Woman Magazine*, a national publication. In August I was written up in the *Washington Post*. Two days ago I received another call from a woman in Washington who is writing an article for a glossy magazine that is published in Washington, D.C. My ideas became public after many years of hard work and putting them into form. My dream of being a writer and having my own office manifested itself during the same period of time. I changed my environment. Now, every time I walk into my office, my subconscious receives a subliminal message of success. This is mine--I dreamed about it, I worked for it, and I finally created it. This is the quintile in action.

Some people may call it talent, some may call it luck. But I don't believe in either of those two words. Talent is something you have developed from doing something over and over until you are better than most at it. Luck is the result of the efforts you have put in for years which eventually becomes manifest in your life. When people say to me, "Aren't you lucky to be a writer; aren't you lucky to have your own office," I just smile and agree with them.

I see the suppression of the quintile as creating a personality who dissipates energy through thoughtless chatter or gossip, as if by discussing the suppressed energy it will magically manifest in the native's life. When it does not manifest, the nerves can suffer. Resentment builds toward those people who are fulfilling the destiny of the planets involved in the quintile in the native's chart.

I have Venus in Libra quintile my ascendant. I used to be suspicious of the "saccharine sweet" personalities who always were involving themselves in other people's lives, wanting to "share" and inject themselves into all their communication. I thought they were phonies. What I didn't realize at the time was that I was suppressing that very part of myself and I resented those people who could carry out what I would have been good at.

What do I do today? I involve myself in other people's lives though consulting, teaching, and lecturing, and I certainly involve myself in your life through my writing. You, the reader, are my friend, someone I can talk to, tell personal anecdotes to illustrating my points, and I know you will understand. I cannot write any other way.

A new editor from New York once began to edit one of my manuscripts. She told me that by the third chapter she stopped trying to edit me out of the book. She realized that was my writing style. And it works for me. Many comments I receive from readers either through the mail or in person stress the point that they feel I am sitting across the kitchen table talking with them over a cup of coffee. I love that because that is how I want you to feel. That is how I communicate what is in my heart. That is my "talent," my quintile, from the Third House of communication (through Venus in Libra, making you feel at home, understanding how you feel, and trying to be fair about what is communicated) to my ascendant, my presence in that communication and my attitude toward life that I convey to you through my writing. I have to be there.

If you look at the quintiles in your chart in the manner I have described above, you may get a better feeling of the true meaning of this aspect. By bringing the energies of the planets involved to fruition through creative thought, you can receive the recognition and status you deserve. Your hidden "talent" will become your visible "talent." You are acknowledged as the public authority in that mode of expression.

According to the foundation laid down by the material in earlier portions of this book, the energy of the points involved in the tredecile is that which lives on after us and affects subsequent generations.

Let's examine this further by looking at the houses in which the tredecile falls on the natural wheel. The tredecile begins at the First House, as always, because it is your view of "reality." The other ends of this aspect fall into the Fourth and Ninth Houses.

The Fourth House is your home and family. It is where you live. Your roots go very deep here, as deep as is possible in this physical world. This house is the foundation of your life and the foundation of the world. The entire chart rests upon the Fourth House. The strength of the world is dependent on the strength of the home and family unit.

This house is where your soul lives in this present incarnation because it is your birth place as well as the circumstances surrounding the end of your current life. The Fourth House is the house of the soul.

The Moon, which naturally rules the Fourth House, contains the accumulation of all past experience. We cannot limit this accumulation of experience to just one incarnation. The Moon rules all your past, your akashic records, your soul memory and experience. You draw upon the experience of your past from the Fourth House.

In the Ninth House the soul experience finds expression in collective thought. In this house we formulate the rules that experience has shown us are necessary in order for society to function as a group mind. The abstract mind comes into play through science, philosophy, and religion where collective ideas are pooled. We begin to see a higher purpose, a vision of a great mental thought pattern beyond our own. The ideas of nations and cultures are affected for hundreds and sometimes thousands of years by what happens in this house.

Look at the effect the ideas of Christianity have had on the moral, economic, social, and political structure of the world for the past two thousand years. Indeed, the power of this house can last for an Age.

Therefore, in the tredecile, you have the capacity to reach into the deepest experience of the energies involved and lift them to great heights of philosophic influence upon the world for many succeeding generations. You can be recognized in your lifetime for this accomplishment--although this is not guaranteed but it will certainly live beyond your life if you carry it to completion. Of course, as with much in your chart, having this aspect does not guarantee this kind of impact or success. It does, however, provide you with the opportunity to create a lasting and meaningful legacy for the planet.

I see the suppression of this energy causing one to become fearful of expressing their deepest feelings. They may decide it is safer to follow the traditional ways of thinking and, as a result, will immerse themselves in "proven" philosophy and collective thought groups where they will not be challenged.

Now that we have discussed the meaning of the quintile and the tredecile, let's examine these aspects between planets and points in some well-known charts. Please take into account that there is not much information currently available on this material, so that what I am presenting here comes from going over my experience with clients over the past fifteen years along with what I perceive as a logical treatment of how the energies should work. I have no statistics to prove what you will find here other than my own experience and common sense. I welcome any comments and observations that you have on any of this material.

Under each chart you will find the following format: Name, Profession, Data, Source, Aspects, and Commentary. The name of the source will be listed under each chart. However, additional information about the source will be listed at the back of this section to eliminate repetition. The charts are set up in Tropical/Placidus style.

To find your quintiles and tredeciles, use the Quintile and Tredecile Chart shown here (on page 80). Since this chart shows the aspects in a counterclockwise direction only, please examine each planet and point in your horoscope when using this chart.

Find the planet or point in question in the column under the arrow. You will find the quintile and tredecile degrees listed to the immediate right of that starting point.

For example, if you have a planet at 5 Aries, the quintile points are 17 Gemini and 23 Capricorn. The tredecile points are 23 Cancer and 17 Sagittarius.

I have designed this chart at five-degree intervals to avoid a cumbersome layout. If you are starting at 7 Aries, simply add two degrees to both quintile and tredecile points.

For example, for a 7 Aries starting point, the quintile points are 19 Gemini and 25 Capricorn and the tredecile points are 25 Cancer and 19 Sagittarius.

In the collection of charts in this section, I have used a three-degree orb in locating the quintile and tredecile.

Plus, in keeping with the feminine nature of this book, I have used the Moon as the starting point of all aspects.

Also, you will find that I use old the glyph ⚥ for Mars instead of the traditional ♂ whose symbol shows the Mars energy gone askew. If we are to bring about a balance of the female and male energies, we need to begin by implanting productive symbols in our collective subconscious. The use of ♀ and ⚥ for Venus and Mars is complementary, depicting the equal and opposite energies of female and male.

I have not analyzed the following charts to any great extent but have suggested some connections as I see them. You most likely will reach conclusions of your own as to the meaning and effectiveness of the quintile and tredecile, which will help in the developmental process of understanding how the aspects fit into any chart.

Finally, following the collection of charts is a section where the personalities in this book plus others are listed under each aspect. Perhaps by comparing the people listed under Moon quintile Uranus, for instance, we can begin to see connecting links between that aspect and the type of individual who has that aspect in her chart.

Hopefully, as more data is compiled, the true effect of the quintile and tredecile will become clearer and more formalized in its interpretation.

Quintile and Tredecile Chart

☿	Q	OO	☿	Q	OO	☿	Q	OO	☿	Q	OO	☿	Q	OO	☿	Q	OO
0	12♊	18♋	0	12♌	18♍	0	12♎	18♏	0	12♐	18♑	0	12♒	18♓	0	12♈	18♉
♈	18♑	12♐	♊	18♓	12♒	♌	18♉	12♈	♎	18♋	12♊	♐	18♍	12♌	♒	18♏	12♎
5	17♊	23♋	5	17♌	23♍	5	17♎	23♏	5	17♐	23♑	5	17♒	23♓	5	17♈	23♉
♈	23♑	17♐	♊	23♓	17♒	♌	23♉	17♈	♎	23♋	17♊	♐	23♍	17♌	♒	23♏	17♎
10	22♊	28♋	10	22♌	28♍	10	22♎	28♏	10	22♐	28♑	10	22♒	28♓	10	22♈	28♉
♈	28♑	22♐	♊	28♓	22♒	♌	28♉	22♈	♎	28♋	22♊	♐	28♍	22♌	♒	28♏	22♎
15	27♊	3♌	15	27♌	3♎	15	27♎	3♐	15	27♐	3♒	15	27♒	3♈	15	27♈	3♊
♈	3♒	27♐	♊	3♈	27♒	♌	3♊	27♈	♎	3♌	27♊	♐	3♎	27♍	♒	3♐	27♎
20	2♋	8♌	20	2♍	8♎	20	2♏	8♐	20	2♑	8♒	20	2♓	8♈	20	2♉	8♊
♈	8♒	2♑	♊	8♈	2♓	♌	8♊	2♉	♎	8♌	2♋	♐	8♎	2♍	♒	8♐	2♏
25	7♋	13♌	25	7♍	13♎	25	7♏	13♐	25	7♑	13♒	25	7♓	13♈	25	7♉	13♊
♈	13♒	7♑	♊	13♈	7♓	♌	13♊	7♉	♎	13♌	7♋	♐	13♎	7♍	♒	13♐	7♏
0	12♋	18♌	0	12♍	18♎	0	12♏	18♐	0	12♑	18♒	0	12♓	18♈	0	12♉	18♊
♉	18♒	12♑	♋	18♈	12♓	♍	18♊	12♉	♏	18♌	12♋	♑	18♎	12♍	♓	18♐	12♏
5	17♋	23♌	5	17♍	23♎	5	17♏	23♐	5	17♑	23♒	5	17♓	23♈	5	17♉	23♊
♉	23♒	17♑	♋	23♈	17♓	♍	23♊	17♉	♏	23♌	17♋	♑	23♎	17♍	♓	23♐	17♏
10	22♋	28♌	10	22♍	28♎	10	22♏	28♐	10	22♑	28♒	10	22♓	28♈	10	22♉	28♊
♉	28♒	22♑	♋	28♈	22♓	♍	28♊	22♉	♏	28♌	22♋	♑	28♎	22♍	♓	28♐	22♏
15	27♋	3♍	15	27♍	3♏	15	27♏	3♑	15	27♑	3♓	15	27♓	3♉	15	27♉	3♋
♉	3♓	27♑	♋	3♉	27♓	♍	3♋	27♉	♏	3♍	27♋	♑	3♏	27♍	♓	3♑	27♏
20	2♌	8♍	20	2♎	8♏	20	2♐	8♑	20	2♒	8♓	20	2♈	8♉	20	2♊	8♋
♉	8♓	2♒	♋	8♉	2♈	♍	8♋	2♊	♏	8♍	2♌	♑	8♏	2♎	♓	8♑	2♐
25	7♌	13♍	25	7♎	13♏	25	7♐	13♑	25	7♒	13♓	25	7♈	13♉	25	7♊	13♋
♉	13♓	7♒	♋	13♉	7♈	♍	13♋	7♊	♏	13♍	7♌	♑	13♏	7♎	♓	13♑	7♐

Forty Astrological Charts as Examples

(with Biographies)

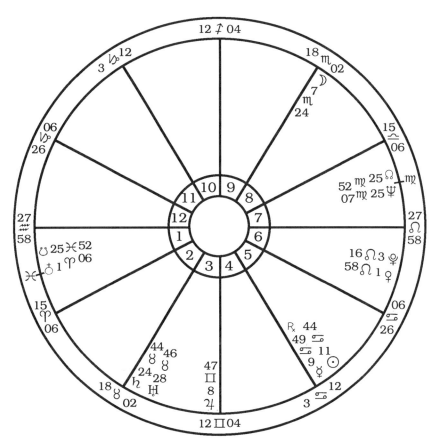

GLORIA ALLRED
lawyer, activist
July 3, 1941
9:56 P.M. E.S.T.
Philadelphia, Pennsylvania
75W10 39N57
(*Profiles of Women*, p. 107)

☉Q♆☊   ☽⊘ASC
♃Q☋   ☉⊘☋
                ♂⊘MC
                ♃⊘♆☊

COMMENTARY: An attorney since 1974, Gloria Allred has fought for rights and housing facilities for battered women and for women in the work force and the military.

"Women are qualified," Allred says. "They understand social issues like unemployment, family problems, crime, and the economy. We want representation." [1]

In 1976 she criticized Governor Jerry Brown of California for his political appointments--84 percent male, 16 percent female--and challenged him to meet with women's groups.

Allred is the head of the Los Angeles National Organization of Women (NOW) and has made over two hundred and fifty television appearances promoting legal and moral issues.

"Women need to gain confidence in their own abilities," says Allred. "I want a better world for my daughter, and women can help make it so." [2]

Her Moon tredecile the Ascendant gives her the personal experience of knowing women's needs. She's been there. And she knows how to fight publicly for those issues with her Mars tredecile the Midheaven. With Jupiter tredecile Neptune, using the legal system to ensure the proper treatment of larger social needs is a natural process for her.

With her Sun quintile the North Node, this may be the first time she has allowed herself to be personally identified with a spearheading effort to accomplish these goals.

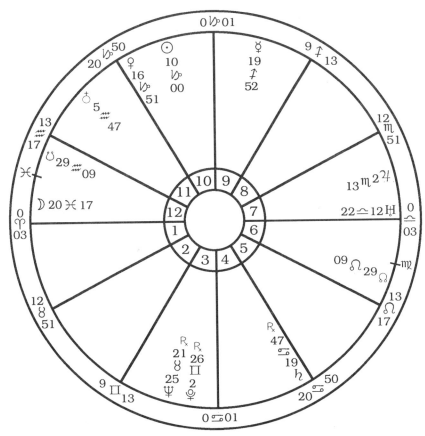

ELIZABETH ARDEN
entrepreneur
December 31, 1886
11:20 A.M. L.M.T.
Toronto, Ontario, Canada
79W22 43N39
(*Profiles of Women*, p. 281)

☽ Q ☉   ☿ ⦿ ♌
☽ Q ♀   ♂ ⦿ ♆
☿ Q ☊   ♄ ⦿ ASC
♀ Q ♃
♀ Q ASC

COMMENTARY: Florence Graham had a brief encounter with nursing and various other jobs before moving from Canada to New York City in 1908. She worked with Eleanor Adair, a beauty specialist, and in 1910 formed a partnership with Elizabeth Hubbard in a Fifth Avenue beauty salon. When they separated, Graham continued the business under the name of Elizabeth Arden. She hired chemists to produce her first two products, face cream and astringent. She eventually would carry over 300 items.

Elizabeth Arden advertised her products as refined in a period when makeup and beauty products were used only by "low women." She was scrupulous and ambitious, ruling every phase of her business. When she died, there were 100 Elizabeth Arden beauty salons throughout the world. She was the best advertisement for her own products, concealing her own age well until her death at the age of eighty-three.

It appears she had an innate understanding of women's needs with her Moon quintile Pluto. With Venus quintile Jupiter, she knew how to capitalize on beauty. Her Mercury aspecting the Nodes suggests her capacity to advertise skillfully.

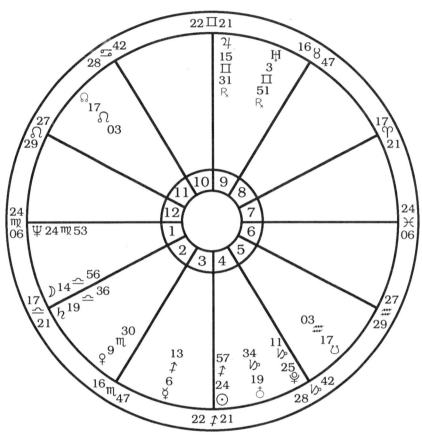

JANE AUSTEN
writer
December 16, 1775
11:45 P.M. L.M.T.
Steveston, Hampshire, England
1W20 51N05
(*Profiles of Women*, p. 260)

☽ Q ☉   ☿ ⦰ ☊

☿ Q Ψ ASC   ♅ ⦰ ☊

☿ Q ☋   ♅ ⦰ ASC

♀ Q ♂

♅ Q ☊

COMMENTARY: Jane Austen was the youngest of seven children, many of whom became distinguished. Until 1801 she lived a quiet domestic life at Steventon, Hampshire, writing mostly for her own pleasure. The family then moved to Bath, and after her father's death, she settled in Chawton, Hampshire. Her stories reflected her background, revolving around upper-middle-class families in the English countryside.

She began writing at an early age and supposedly wrote humorous compositions before age of 16. *Pride and Prejudice* was written when she was 21 years old, but was not published until she was 38. She wrote five other novels although they were not especially popular during her lifetime. Sir Walter Scott, however, praised them highly for their excellence.

"Today they are regarded as among the best novels in the language....The reason for their high place appears to lie in Miss Austen's skill as a storyteller and a drawer of character....As a storyteller, she has, in...technical construction, no superior." [3]

The Moon quintile the Sun may have given her the opportunity to indulge her self-development in a nurturing home atmosphere.

Certainly her skill as a weaver of stories is suggested by Mercury quintile Neptune and the Ascendant. It also indicates her imagination and sense of the humorous.

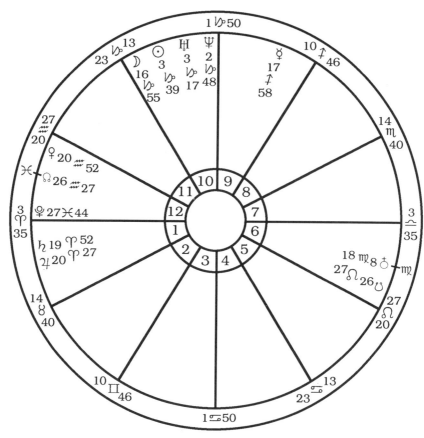

CLARA BARTON
founder of American Red Cross
December 25, 1821
11:40 A.M. E.S.T.
Oxford, Massachusetts
71W52 42N08
(*Profiles of Women*, p. 272)

☽ ☿ ♀   ☿ ☾ ASC
            ♃ ♄ ☽ ☉ ♅ ♆ MC

COMMENTARY: Clara Barton began as a teacher, then became a clerk in a patent office in Washington. When the Civil War broke out, she volunteered to work as a nurse in the hospitals on the battlefield.

She was put in charge of the hospitals at one front, and was there during a number of battles. She then began to search for missing Union soldiers and, in 1865, was placed in charge of this search by President Lincoln.

Because of her aid in the Franco-Prussian War in 1879, she was decorated with the Gold Cross of Remembrance of Baden and the Iron Cross of Merit of Germany.

She was president of the American Red Cross Society in 1881. Her suggestion amended the rules of the Red Cross allowing relief not only in war but during calamities such as flood, earthquakes, famine, and pestilence. She travelled to Turkey, Cuba, Spain, and many other countries assisting during such calamities. She wrote a number of publications and resigned from the Society in 1904.

Barton's work on the battlefields of the Civil War and the Franco-Prussian War seem to be indicated by her Moon quintile Pluto. Her American Red Cross work shows a social awareness of the universality of all life, evident in Jupiter tredecile Neptune. She certainly enlightened the world--through Jupiter tredecile Uranus--to the need of those in desperate conditions.

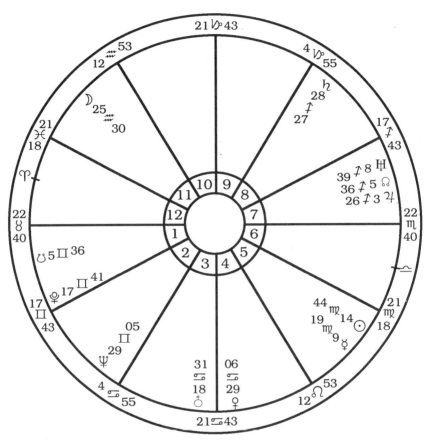

TAYLOR CALDWELL
writer
September 7, 1900
8:37 P.M. G.M.T.
Manchester, England
2W15 53N30
(*Profiles of Women*, p. 174)
☿♀♆   ☿☽♄

COMMENTARY: Taylor Caldwell emigrated to the United States in 1907. At nine years of age, she began to write and illustrate her own books. She also was talented in painting and sculpture, but rather than scattering her abilities, she decided to concentrate on writing. Because her father disapproved of education for women, she took evening sessions and graduated at age 31 from the University of Buffalo in 1931. She and her second husband wrote a number of best-selling novels starting with *Dynasty of Death* in 1938.

Her own books, including *This Side of Innocence*, *The Devil's Advocate*, *Dear and Glorious Physician*, and *The Captain And The Kings*, were intricately plotted. She wrote suspenseful narratives with great vitality. She was called a "storyteller par excellence."

Her Mercury is highlighted by being the only planet with connections. The tredecile to Saturn shows the detailed structure of her work and the quintile to Neptune depicts the storyteller par excellence, one whose imagination painted word pictures of times in which she had no apparent contact.

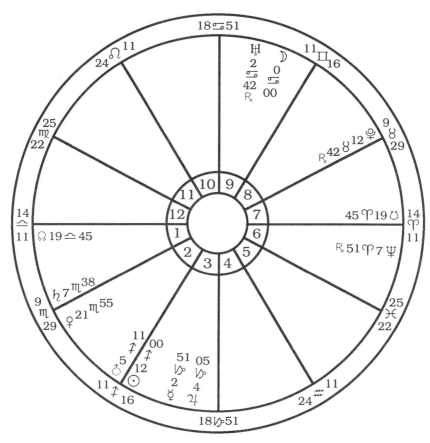

EDITH CAVELL
nurse
December 4, 1865
2:30 A.M. L.M.T.
Swardeston, Norfolk, England
1E15 52N35
(*Profiles of Women*, p. 254)

☽♅Q☊   ☽♅⊙☊
☿♃Q☊   ☿♃⊙☊

COMMENTARY: Edith Cavell was an English nurse who was executed in 1915 during the German occupation of Belgium.

She was a trained nurse working at a clinic in Belgium at the time World War I broke out. Although she was in England at that time, she returned to Belgium and converted the clinic into a hospital for wounded soldiers. She was left in charge of the hospital during the German occupation, nursing soldiers from both sides of the war. With her friends she secretly helped allied soldiers across enemy lines to rejoin their armies and assisted Belgians of military age to evade German capture.

She was turned in by a Belgian traitor (who was found murdered a year later) and was kept in solitary confinement although British, Spanish, and American authorities tried to intervene. At two in the morning on October 12, 1915, she fearlessly faced a firing squad. Before she died she told a British chaplain, "I have seen death so often that it is not strange or fearful to me. Standing as I do in view of God and eternity, I realize that patriotism is not enough. I must have no hatred or bitterness toward anyone."

Her monument stands today in Trafalgar Square in London. Cavell's Moon, Mercury, Jupiter, and Uranus contacting her North and South Nodes, suggest a nurturing destiny, one certainly fraught with danger and unusual circumstances.

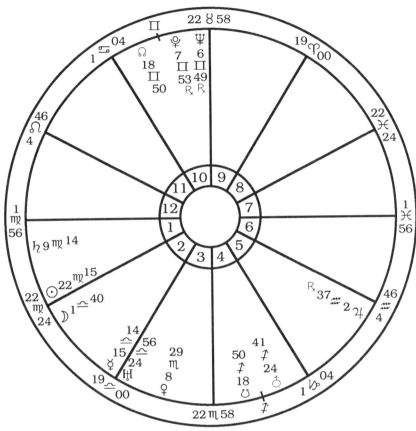

AGATHA CHRISTIE
writer
September 15, 1890
4:00 A.M. G.M.T.
Torquay, England
3W30 50N30
(*Profiles of Women*, p. 178)

☿ ♀ ♂   ⊙ ☽ ♆ ♀

☊ ♀ ASC   ☿ ☽ ♃

                ♂ ☽ ♄

                ☊ ☽ ASC

COMMENTARY: Agatha Christie was an English detective-story writer. After a private education she studied music in Paris. In 1914 she married Colonel Archibald Christie, from whom she was divorced in 1928. In 1930 she married again, this time to archaeologist Max Mallowan, and traveled with him on several archaeological digs to Syria and Iraq.

Her first detective story, *The Mysterious Affair at Styles*, and many that subsequently followed, gained her international recognition. Her main character, Hercule Poirot, the fastidious Belgian detective with his tight shoes and "little grey cells" became as well known as Sherlock Holmes. Agatha Christie also created Miss Marple, the deceptively simple elderly country woman, who exposed many perpetrators of crime.

Miss Christie's Mercury tredecile Jupiter allowed her writings to capture the imagination of people from all countries and to leave an enduring imprint. Might not her Mars tredecile Saturn in Virgo describe the fastidious Poirot with the "little grey cells" and the tight shoes?

A number of films have been made from her books, indicating the effects of the Sun tredecile Neptune.

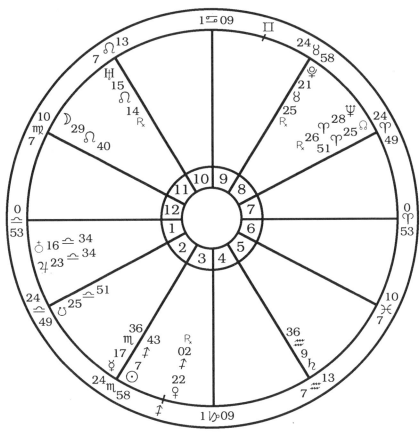

WINSTON CHURCHILL
statesman
November 30, 1874
1:30 A.M. L.M.T.
Woodstock, England
1W15 51N45
(*American Book of Charts* and
*The Golden Home and High School
Encyclopedia*, volume 4, p. 588)

COMMENTARY: Winston Churchill entered politics in 1900 as a conservative. In 1904 he broke with the party over tariff questions and joined the liberals.

As time went on he held many posts, becoming increasingly conservative in his political views once more. He eventually became Prime Minister of England, and was made an honorary United States citizen in 1963 by an act of Congress.

His career had the bigger-than-life quality of an epic. But Winston Churchill was a warm and very human being. No one was stronger in loyalty to friends, quicker to be moved to tears or to bubble with laughter...he was deeply involved in all the great affairs of the century....Indeed it is impossible to talk for long of the twentieth century without speaking his name.... [4]

A last tribute, from former Prime Minister Harold Macmillan, said it all: "The life of the man whom we are today honoring is unique. The oldest among us can recall nothing to compare with it and the younger ones among you, however long you live, will never see the like again." [5]

The bigger-than-life quality of this man is shown through Jupiter tredecile the Midheaven. Mars tredecile the Midheaven was evident during the Second World War when he rallied his people during the German bombings of his country. He was their courage and their faith (Jupiter). His was a destiny of uniqueness (Uranus tredecile the North Node), a life of which we may "never see the like again."

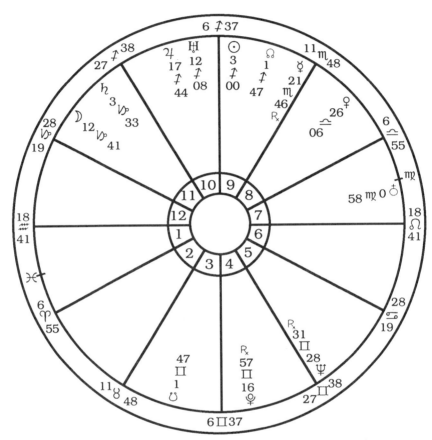

HELEN GAHAGAN DOUGLAS
congresswoman
November 25, 1900
12:00 noon E.S.T.
Boonton, New Jersey
74W25 40N54
(*Profiles of Women*, p. 246)
ASC ♃ MC ♂ ☽ ♃

COMMENTARY: Helen Gahagan Douglas was voted one of the twelve most beautiful women in America. Although she began her career as an actress (she was married to Melvyn Douglas, her leading man in a film in 1930) and sang light opera in Europe and America, she soon found that her awareness of the social aspects of the world began to push into the foreground of her life. She eventually turned away from the theater and toward politics.

This turn of affairs was the result of living through the depression and watching the rise of Nazism in Europe while she toured. She began her political work at the grass-roots level for the Democratic State Committee in 1941 and by July 1944 was a delegate to the Democratic National Convention. She eventually served as California's representative to Congress for three terms.

Perhaps her beauty gave her the public attention through the Ascendant quintile the Midheaven she needed in order to pursue the driving need to make a difference in the social order with Mars tredecile Jupiter.

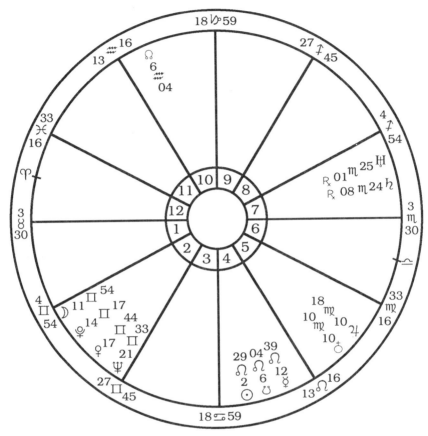

AMELIA EARHART
pilot
July 24, 1897
11:30 P.M. C.S.T.
Atchison, Kansas
95W08 39N32
(*Profiles of Women*, p. 131)

COMMENTARY: Amelia Earhart was lost over the Pacific, and presumably died, on July 3, 1937.

In 1928 she was the first woman to fly across the Atlantic; in 1932 she was the first to fly the Atlantic alone and to make a nonstop flight across the United States; in 1935 she was the first to fly from Hawaii to the States. She was the first woman to receive the Distinguished Flying Cross.

On June 1, 1937, she and co-pilot Fred Noonan left Miami, Florida, to fly around the world. They proceeded without mishap to South America, Africa, India, and Australia. They left New Guinea on July 1 to cross 2,550 miles of open ocean to Howland Island in the Pacific. During that time, radio messages of distress, thought to have been sent from Amelia Earhart's plane, were received. Although the greatest rescue search in the history of aviation took place, no trace of the plane or the pilots was ever found. She was declared legally dead in 1939.

With all these accomplishments in aviation, one certainly would expect an emphasis on the planet Uranus, and indeed she has Mars quintile Uranus, Jupiter quintile Uranus, and Uranus quintile and tredecile the North and South Nodes.

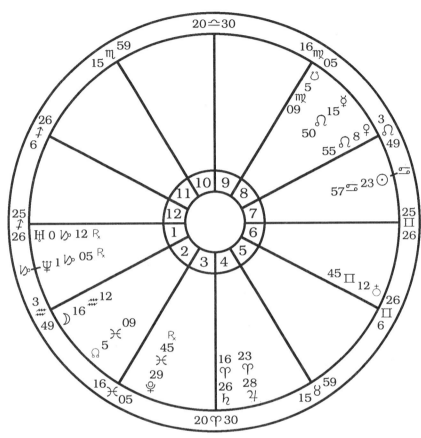

MARY BAKER EDDY
founder of Christian Science
July 16, 1821
5:38 P.M. L.M.T.
Bow, New Hampshire
71W32 43N08
(*Profiles of Women*, p. 120)

☽ Q ♃   ☿ ⊙ ♃
♀ Q MC   ☿ ⊙ ♄
☊ Q ♇

COMMENTARY: Mary Baker Eddy was the sixth and youngest child of Abigail and Mark Baker. Her ancestors figured importantly in American history and her immediate family was prominent. She was raised in a home of refinement and religious devotion.

She was frail and subject to illness, which kept her from regular school attendance. When she was 15, one of her tutors was Rev. Enoch Corser, pastor at the Congregational Church in Tilton, New Hampshire. He died before she became famous, but his son wrote of her:

...I well remember her gift of expression, which was very marked...my father held her in the highest esteem...he considered her, even at an early age, superior both intellectually and spiritually to any other woman in Tilton. He predicted for Mrs. Eddy a great future and spoke of her as an intellectual and spiritual genius. [6]

She wrote articles and poems that were published, and in 1875 printed the textbook of Christian Science, *Science and Health with Key to the Scriptures*. Recognizing the need for a church to support her philosophy, she organized the First Church of Christ, Scientist, in Boston in 1879. In 1883 she began the first of the Christian Science periodicals.

Her "gift of expression" is evident in Mercury tredecile Jupiter and Saturn. Her Moon quintile Jupiter bestows the imagination and feeling that came from her soul.

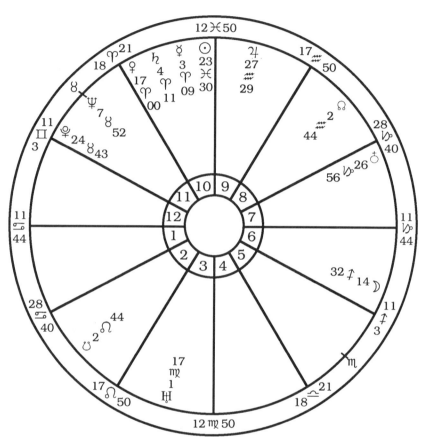

ALBERT EINSTEIN
scientist
March 14, 1879
11:30 A.M. L.M.T.
Ulm, Germany
10E00 48N30
(*American Book of Charts*)

☽Q♃   ☽◎☿♄
♃Q♆

COMMENTARY: Albert Einstein was born of middle-class Jewish parents. He discovered Euclidean geometry at the age of 12, and began to read voraciously so that by the age of 16 he had a good understanding of calculus and classical physics. But he disliked traditional education with its narrow concern for rules and examinations. He graduated from the Federal Institute of Technology in Zurich, Switzerland, in 1900.

He taught high school for a while because he was unable to obtain a university position. While an examiner at the Swiss patent office in Bern from 1902 to 1909 (an intensely creative period), he published three papers, the third of which contained the theory of relativity. (The first complete publication of this work came out in 1916.)

With these publications at age 26, he emerged as one of the greatest scientists in history. He received his Ph.D. from the University of Zurich in 1905.

The Theory of General Relativity was his greatest accomplishment and one of the "greatest achievements of the human mind." On November 10, 1922, he received the Nobel Prize for physics. Thereafter he began his search for a unified field theory.

He was not a religious man in the usual sense, but he had a firm belief in the order of the universe. "The most incomprehensible thing about the world," he said, "is that it is comprehensible." [7]

It is said in some circles that Einstein was a mystic, that he gained much of his information from imaginary trips on rockets and by talking with the flowers in his garden. Certainly his Moon quintile Jupiter and Jupiter quintile Neptune leans toward this kind of mental flight. The ability to construct form from his mental meanderings shows in Moon tredecile Saturn.

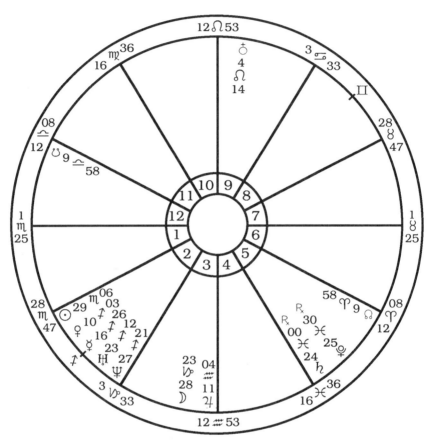

"GEORGE ELIOT"
MARY ANN EVANS
writer
November 22, 1819
5:00 A.M. L.M.T.
Nuneaton, England
1W30 52N33
(*Profiles of Women*, p. 241)

☽Q☊   ☽⦻℧
☉Q♃   ☉⦻☊
☉Q℧   ♅⦻☊
♅Q℧

COMMENTARY: A distinguished English novelist, Mary Ann Evans spent her first 21 years in a "cheerful red-brick, ivy covered house," among people and scenes she later would immortalize. Her beloved mother died when she was 17, followed by her sister's marriage. Hence, the household duties fell upon her. A voracious reader, she learned Italian, Greek, German, and Latin. She attended her father from 1842 through recurring illness until his death in 1849.

She then became sub-editor of *Westminster Review*. During this time she met George Henry Lewes, who would have a lasting influence upon her as a business manager, critic, mentor, and companion. Her articles began to appear under his encouragement. Three stories followed in book form in 1858 under the pen name of George Eliot. Critics like William Thackeray and Charles Dickens recognized literary greatness. Since impostors began to claim authorship of her work, she revealed the fact that she and George Eliot were one in the same.

In 1871 she received an unheard-of sum of 7,000 pounds for her historical romance, *Romola*. This book reflected the author's "power of characterization." Some critics feel that her best novel is *Daniel Deronda*, although it was not as popular as some of her others.

Her "power of characterization" could show through the Sun quintile Jupiter and tredecile the Midheaven, the Midheaven indicating the public's recognition of her definition of the self in the Sun and Jupiter's connections with the collective thought patterns.

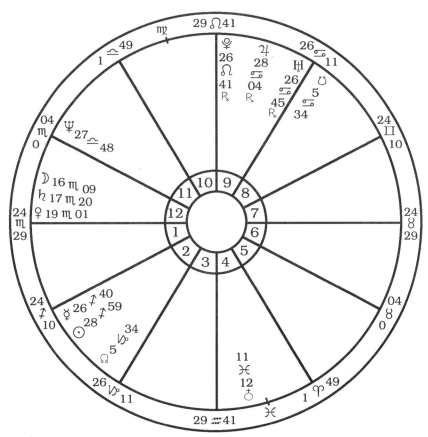

CHRIS EVERT
tennis champion
December 21, 1954
4:30 A.M. E.S.T.
Fort Lauderdale, Florida
80W08 26N07
(*Profiles of Women*, p. 266)
☽♀♄☉♃♅
♂♍ASC

COMMENTARY: Chris Evert, one of five children in a family who enjoyed tennis, began to make a name for herself at the age of 15 when she beat Australia's Margaret Court in Charlotte, North Carolina, in the fall of 1970. In April 1971 she won the Virginia Slims Masters in St. Petersburg, Florida, and in August was chosen to compete in Ohio for the Whitman Cup, the youngest player ever to do so. She crushed Virginia Wade, Britain's best player.

On her eighteenth birthday, Chris Evert turned professional thus becoming eligible for prize money. In January 1973 her name graced a line of tennis ensembles.

Slim and graceful at five-feet-five inches, Evert captured the imagination of the crowds who cheered when she won and cheered when her opponents made mistakes. Because of her beaming smile and soft voice, she was called Little Miss Sunshine, Cinderella in Sneakers, Miss Charisma, and America's Sweetheart. She retired from the game in September 1989 and undoubtedly will be remembered as one of tennis's best and best-loved champions.

Perhaps her Moon and Venus tredecile Jupiter accounts for her charisma and popularity with the crowd as well as her grace on the court. Mars tredecile the Ascendant gives her the stamina to endure the grueling hours on the court.

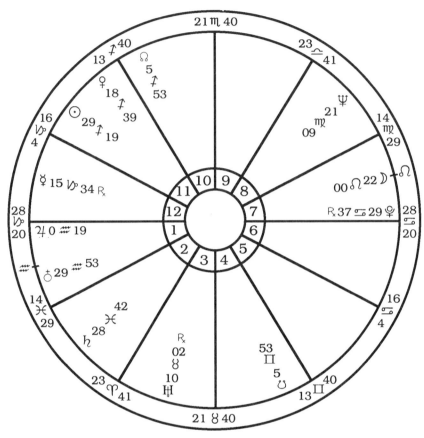

JANE FONDA
actress
December 21, 1937
9:14 A.M. E.S.T.
Manhattan, New York
73W59 40N46
(*Profiles of Women*, p. 265)

☿ Q ♄   Ψ ⦾ ☊
♀ Q ♂
♂ Q ♅
Ψ Q ☊

COMMENTARY: Jane Fonda is the daughter of late film actor Henry Fonda. She dropped out of Vassar College and studied painting and languages in Paris, modelled in New York, and made her Broadway debut in 1960 in *There Was a Little Girl*. This brought her recognition as well as her first film in 1960, *Tall Story*.

Her dramatic abilities came through in the film *They Shoot Horses, Don't They?* She won academy awards as best actress in *Klute* (1972) and *Coming Home* (1977). Some of her other films include *Julia*, *The China Syndrome*, and *On Golden Pond*, in which she starred with her father.

During the Vietnam War she was censured by the United States State Department for requesting over Radio Hanoi that the American pilots stop their bombing raids. In 1972 she divorced French film director Roger Vadim and married Tom Hayden, an antiwar activist.

Her Mercury quintile Saturn and Mars quintile Uranus certainly suggest her serious attitude and ability to stir things up. With Jupiter quintile the Midheaven, she is idealistic about a larger social order for the world.

HELEN FRANKENTHALER
artist
December 12, 1928
11:30 P.M. E.S.T.
New York, New York
73W57 40N45
(*Profiles of Women*, p. 258)

♅♀MC   ☉☿♄◐♆
☋♀ASC   ☿◐♅
             ♌◐ASC

COMMENTARY: Helen Frankenthaler studied at Bennington College and was noticed by the age of 24. She was influenced early by cubists Kandinsky and Miro; American painters Dove, Marin, and Gorky; and later by abstract expressionists like Jackson Pollock. By 1952 her work had matured through absorption of these techniques. In the 1970s she was recognized as a leading contemporary abstract painter. She produced fresh, original shapes and won international acclaim. She married painter Robert Motherwell in 1958.

Her unorthodox style of dripping paints on canvas, soaking unprimed canvas with diluted pigments, and working with a rag or her feet produced bold images, splashes of paint that flowed freely. Her work is displayed in major art galleries and some pieces sell for $30,000 each.

Uranus, the planet of originality and unorthodoxy, and Neptune, the planet of free form, aspect her Sun, Mercury, and Saturn. Venus, the art planet, is not aspected here, although her original way of looking at the world and her ability to translate the formless images she sees is artistic.

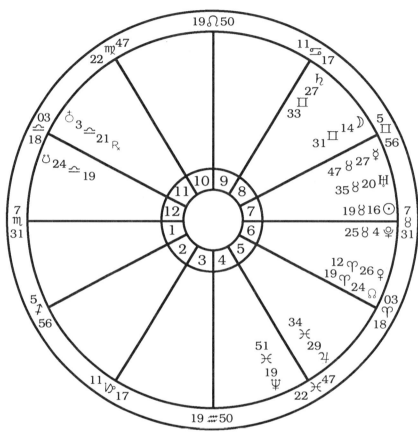

SIGMUND FREUD
psychoanalyst
May 6, 1856
6:30 P.M. L.M.T.
Frieberg (Pribor), Germany
18E09 49N38
(*American Book of Charts*)

☽Q♃   ☽⦻♂
          ♀⦻MC

COMMENTARY: The father of psychoanalysis, Sigmund Freud was a "pioneer in the field of subconscious exploration." [8] Freud is noted for the concept of psychoanalysis, one of the important ideas of this century that reaches beyond psychiatry into the social sciences and the arts.

Born of middle-class Jewish parents, he was three years old when the family moved to Vienna, where he lived for 79 years.

He joined the medical faculty of the University of Vienna in 1873 and distinguished himself as a medical student. He acquired full training in all branches of medicine but concentrated on psychiatry.

In 1902 Freud formed a group that met regularly to study his investigations. Among them were Alfred Adler and Wilhelm Stekel, and in 1906 he met Carl Jung. But between 1911 and 1914, all three had dissociated from Freud because of personal and scientific matters.

Some of Freud's work was explained in his books and papers. *The Interpretation of Dreams* expounded his belief that the study of the unconscious mind could be done through dreams. He also proposed a tripartite division of consciousness into id, ego, and superego.

In 1930 his literary abilities brought him the Goethe Prize, which he treasured. In 1938 he was forced to flee Vienna because of the Nazis and spent his last few years in England.

A "pioneer in the field of subconscious exploration" is a perfect description of Freud's Moon tredecile Mars and his Moon quintile Jupiter helps as well.

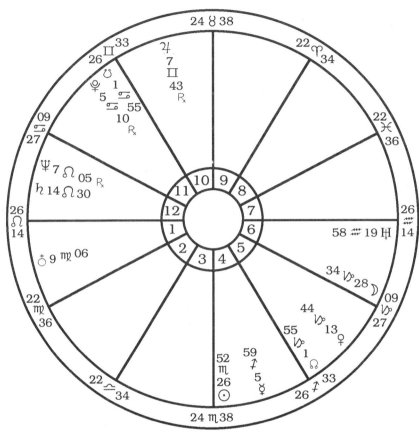

INDIRA GANDHI
Prime Minister of India
November 19, 1917
11:39 P.M. 1st Zone 5.5
Allahabad, India
81E50 24N27
(*Profiles of Women*, p. 235)

☿ Q ♅   ☉ ⊙ ♆
♆ Q MC   ♃ ⊙ ♅

COMMENTARY: The daughter of Jawaharlal Nehru, prime minister of India, Indira grew up knowing most of the leaders in the struggle for independence from Britain. For nearly 18 years she was her father's hostess and confidante.

In March of 1942 she married Feroze Gandhi (no relation to Mohandas K. "Mahatma" Gandhi), a journalist she had known in her childhood. Six months later they were arrested for their involvement in the nationalist movement. They were released in 1943 and returned to Allahabad where their two sons, Rajiv and Sanjay, were born.

In 1955 Indira became involved in the Congress party and was elected president four years later. Her political career began. She dominated Indian politics for 20 years, becoming prime minister in 1966.

She took "extraordinary steps" when, in June 1975, a high court judge ruled she must stay out of politics for six years because of election abuses. Imposing a state of emergency, she used measures that were alleged violations of the constitution. After a few bumpy years of expulsion and repudiation from the voters, she won a landslide victory in the January 1980 election.

She was assassinated on October 31, 1984, by Sikh extremists, members of her special security force.

With Mercury quintile Uranus and Jupiter tredecile Uranus, she had a brilliant mind and strong social insights. Her Sun tredecile Neptune suggest an illusionary picture of the real woman, but one who was familiar with power in circles filled with diverse religious groups.

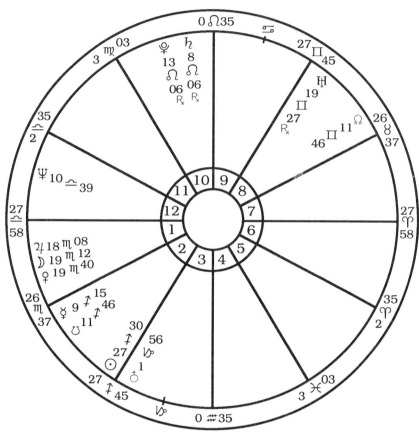

URI GELLER
telekenic
December 20, 1946
2:00 A.M. E.E.T.
Tel Aviv, Palestine
34E49 32N02
(*American Book of Charts*)

♀ ☿ ASC
☽ ♀ ♃ ⊙ MC

COMMENTARY: The handsome six-feet two-inch, 170-pound Uri Geller, with his piercing eyes and thick dark hair, is known for his alleged feats of clairvoyance and telepathy as well as feats of psychokinesis, using the mind to influence objects. He is said to bend or break metal objects such as knives and keys through mental concentration.

In his autobiography, *Uri Geller: My Story*, he tells that at the age of four he was playing alone when there was a high-pitched sound in his ears. Everything else stopped as if time stood still. He then saw a light coming toward him which was not the sun. He felt as if he had been knocked over, with a pain in his forehead. He fell unconscious for an underdetermined time. When he awoke, he ran home to tell him mother because he knew something important had occurred. Geller's mother states that from that time, he seemed able to read her mind and know how she had done at playing cards. His family hoped he would outgrow this strange ability.

He spent time in the military and then signed with a manager to become an entertainer. He had standing-room-only audiences.

Uri Geller has been tested by scientists and magicians.

Opinions vary as to his abilities. He still claims things come to him in strange ways, like his poetry. He feels he is an instrument for a higher power.

With Pluto quintile the Ascendant, he has physical access to deeper powers. With the Moon, Venus, Saturn, and Neptune aspecting his Midheaven, he would capture the public's attention.

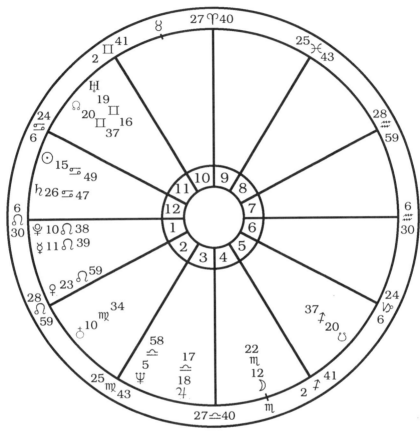

CYNTHIA GREGORY
ballerina
July 8, 1946
6:32 A.M. P.S.T.
Los Angeles, California
118W15 34N04
(*Profiles of Women*, p. 112)

COMMENTARY: Cynthia Gregory is an American ballerina noted for her "technical perfection and lyrical grace." En pointe, she is six-feet one-inches tall .

She started ballet lessons at the age of five and it soon became apparent that she was beyond the children's classes. When she was fifteen, her noted dance instructor, Jacques d'Ambroise, recommended her to the San Francisco Ballet where she was promoted to soloist within months.

In 1965 she joined the American Ballet Theatre and became the lead dancer in 1967. She danced the lead in Nureyev's *Raymonda* in 1975 (he called her "America's prima ballerina absoluta") and Baryshnikov's *Cinderella* in 1984. Gregory received a *Dance Magazine* award in 1975.

Certainly her "technical perfection and lyrical grace" is shown by Saturn tredecile Neptune. The emotional stamina required for her rigorous routine and the ensuing perfection in her work shows in the Moon tredecile Saturn. Neptune aspecting her nodes may indicate her destiny with dance.

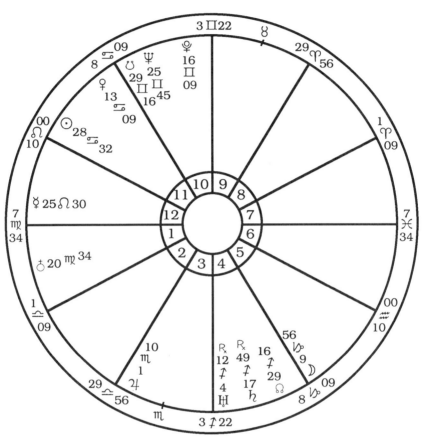

ERNEST HEMINGWAY
writer, adventurer
July 21, 1899
8:00 A.M. C.S.T.
Oak Park, Illinois
87W47 41N53
(*American Book of Charts*)

COMMENTARY: Ernest Hemingway began as a newspaper reporter. During World War I he went to Italy as a Red Cross ambulance driver, and subsequently volunteered in the Italian Army, where he was wounded seriously. These war experiences gave him the material used in *A Farewell To Arms*. This book, along with *The Sun Also Rises* and *For Whom The Bell Tolls*, express his war-weary feelings.

In 1920 he met Sherwood Anderson, a man he admired greatly. In December 1921 he went to Europe as a roving correspondent for the *Toronto Star* and in Paris met Ezra Pound and Gertrude Stein, who became his literary mentors.

Hemingway chose an adventurous and often dangerous way of living. His writing was filled with action, violence, and death.

In 1953 he received the Pulitzer Prize for *The Old Man and the Sea*, which was cited in the Nobel Prize for Literature he won in 1954.

He died of a gunshot wound on July 2, 1961 in Ketchum, Idaho.

His involvement and preoccupation with war and violence may be indicated through the Moon tredecile Mars and Mars quintile Uranus. He used these experiences as the background for his literature.

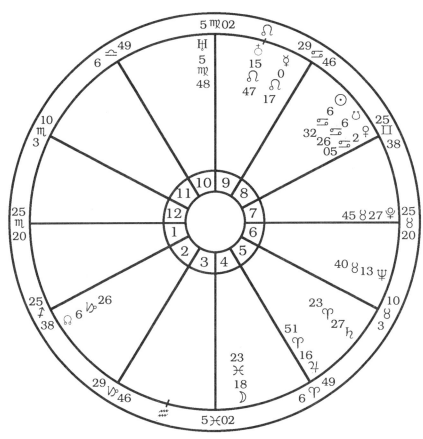

HELEN KELLER
educator
June 27, 1880
4:02 P.M. L.M.T.
Tuscumbia, Alabama
87W42 34N44
(*Profiles of Women*, p. 103)

COMMENTARY: Helen Keller was stricken deaf and blind when she was about two years old. When she was six, she became the student of Anne Sullivan, a teacher from Boston's Perkins Institute for the Blind. Miss Sullivan taught Helen to see with her fingertips and hear with her hands and feet.

Helen's first step in understanding speech and her environment came on the day when Miss Sullivan was spelling the word "water" on her hand while water was flowing over her other hand.

Helen Keller learned quickly. In three years, she knew the manual and braille alphabets and could read and write. In 1890 she took speech lessons with Sarah Fuller. She studied lip training, arithmetic, geography, French and German at the Wright-Humanson School for the Deaf in New York, and subsequently went to the Cambridge School for Young Ladies and Radcliffe College. She graduated with honors in 1904. Anne Sullivan was always at her side, interpreting classes, lectures, and books.

Helen Keller began to study the problems of the blind. She spent many years touring the United States, Europe, and Asia to speak for the handicapped, and eventually started the Helen Keller Endowment Fund for the American Foundation for the Blind.

She wrote many articles and books including *Let Us Have Faith.*

Miss Keller's chart is filled with quintiles and tredeciles. Mercury and Mars quintile Pluto suggests overcoming great odds to communicate. She became an example of the success over restriction through the Sun quintile Saturn.

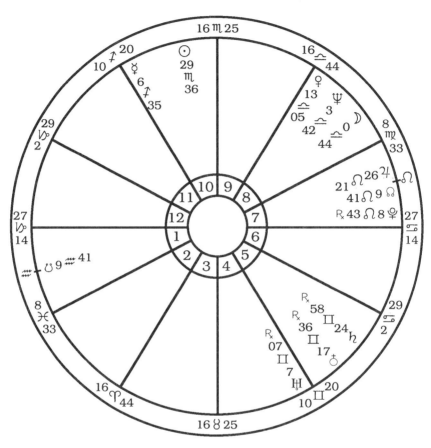

BILLIE JEAN KING
tennis champion
November 22, 1943
11:45 A.M. P.W.T.
Long Beach, California
118W11 33N47
(*Profiles of Women*, p. 242)

☉♀☊   ☉☽♀☊
            ♀☽♄
            ♂☽♆

COMMENTARY: Billie Jean King won numerous tennis champion-ships and paved the way for equality of women in tournament prizes. In 1971 she became the first woman athlete to earn more than $100,000 in one year. She worked hard at her sport and by age 33 had won 19 titles at Wimbledon. In a highly publicized "Battle of the Sexes," she soundly beat ex-champion Bobby Riggs, who had claimed that men's tennis was far superior to women's. She was the leading player of her generation.

She had a series of knee and heel operations and, in 1977, her knee was still painful a year after surgery. She gave up her title to Chris Evert in Palm Springs.

Billie Jean Moffit married Larry King while they were students at Los Angeles State College. By 1977 she and her husband were promoting their various business interests.

She has been quoted as saying she is not competitive but rather a perfectionist, perhaps suggested by Venus tredecile Saturn. Her personal involvement in the transformation of the sport she loves is shown by the Sun tredecile Pluto.

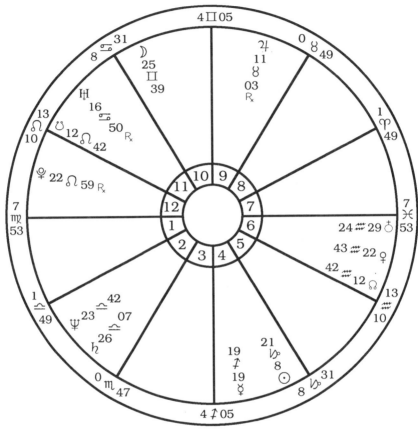

GELSEY KIRKLAND
ballerina
December 29, 1952
9:36 P.M. E.S.T.
Fountain Hill, Pennsylvania
75W24 40N37
(*Profiles of Women*, p. 280)

☽ ♀ ASC   ♄ ♆ ⊗ ☊
☉ ♀ ♄ ♆
♂ ♀ ♃
♄ ♆ ♀ ☋

COMMENTARY: Five-foot four-inch, 97-pound Gelsey Kirkland is small-boned and delicate. Her father wanted his daughters to be actresses, but her mother won out with dance at the New York City Ballet's School of American Ballet. Gelsey accompanied her sister to classes and at age eight began taking classes herself. At age 15 she was a member of the New York City Ballet's corps de ballet. She was a soloist at 17 and a principal dancer at 19. She left the company in 1974.

Mikhail Baryshnikov called her shortly after his defection from Russia to the United States and asked her to be his partner in the American Ballet Theatre, his company in the United States. She won glowing reviews for her technically demanding grand pas de deux.

She impressed audiences with her lightness and impeccable timing. One critic wrote that her equilibrium was incredible in off-balance postures.

Her Saturn aspects suggest her impeccable timing; Mars quintile Jupiter accounts for her equilibrium, an aspect, often accompanied by Pluto, sometimes found in the charts of athletes.

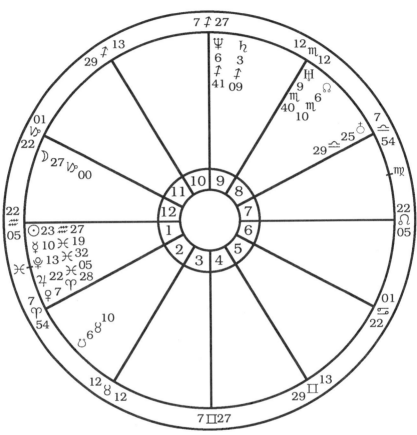

ABRAHAM LINCOLN
16th president of the United States
February 12, 1809
6:45 A.M. L.M.T.
Hodgenville, Kentucky
85W45 37N33
(*American Book of Charts*)

☽☿♀   ☉ASC☾♅☊
☉ASC☌☋   ♃☾♄(♆MC)

COMMENTARY: Abraham Lincoln came from humble beginnings. In his early years he worked as a clerk, managed a mill, split rails, acted as village postmaster, and held a number of odd jobs while he studied law.

He became interested in politics and subsequently was elected to Congress for the 1847-1849 term. He then joined the new Republican party in 1856.

In 1860 he became the Republican candidate for the U. S. Senate against Stephen A. Douglas, senator from Illinois. He argued against the extension of slavery into other areas of the country because he thought this would cause the institution to die out. He lost the election but became a nationally known figure. Later that year he became the Republican candidate for president and won election to the White House as the nation's sixteenth president.

Lincoln, determined to preserve the Union, gave the secession movement in the South momentum because the South regarded him as a threat to slavery. The Civil War broke out. The emancipation of the slaves occurred in 1863 and the war was over in 1865. Lincoln was planning reconstruction of the country based on moderation when he was assassinated at Ford's Theater by John Wilkes Booth on April 14, 1865.

Lincoln's concern with the preservation of the Union may show in his Moon quintile Venus, and the need to keep the family together and operating harmoniously. Jupiter tredecile Saturn is a sense of the right person at the right time with the right ideas.

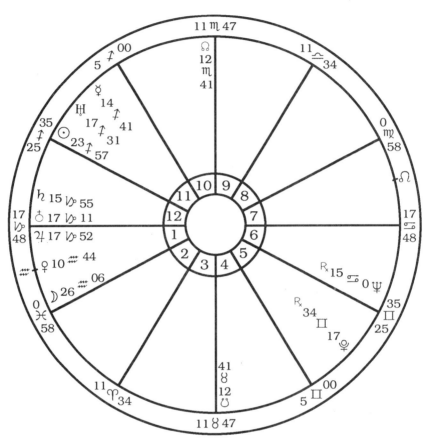

MARGARET MEAD
anthropologist
December 16, 1901
9:00 A.M. E.S.T.
Philadelphia, Pennsylvania
75W10 39N57
(*Profiles of Women*, p. 261)

☽♀☿♅   ☽◎☊MC
☽♀☋

COMMENTARY: With her Ph.D. from Columbia University in 1929, Margaret Mead began to study the primitive peoples of the South Seas. Her first anthropological field work in Samoa from 1925 to 1926 resulted in the publication of *Coming of Age in Samoa,* where she showed that adolescents grow to adulthood in Samoa without the accompanying crises characteristic of Western society.

She was interested in the relationship between personality and culture, concentrating on infant and child care and adolescent and sexual behavior. The family was a prime focus.

She studied national character, resulting in the publications *And Keep Your Powder Dry,* about American culture, and *Soviet Attitudes Towards Authority.*

During World War II she was executive secretary of the committee on food habits of the National Research Council. In 1956-1957 she served as president of the World Federation for Mental Health and was president of the American Anthropological Association for 1959-1960.

Of her own relationships, she said, "I have had three very successful marriages. Good work came of each of them and I am on good terms with all three husbands to this day."[9]

Mead's emphasis on infants, child care, and adolescents certainly is depicted in all the aspects to her Moon, the only planet in her chart that is aspected in this way.

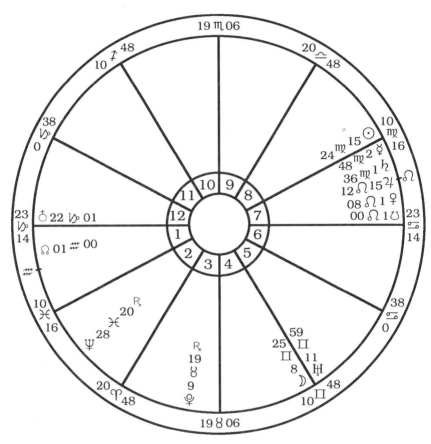

"GRANDMA MOSES"
ANNA MARY ROBERTSON
primitive painter
September 7, 1860
3:58 P.M. L.M.T.
Greenwich, New York
73W30 43N05
(*Profiles of Women*, p. 173)

☽ ♅ ☊ ♆   ♀ ⊙ MC
☊ ☿ MC   ♂ ASC ⊙ ♀
            ☋ ⊙ MC

COMMENTARY: "Grandma Moses" was born on a farm in Greenwich, New York. She had only months of education during her childhood summers, and left at the age of 13 to work as a hired girl. She married Thomas Moses in 1887 and lived new Staunton, Virginia, until 1905, when they bought a farm near Eagle Bridge, New York. There she spent the remainder of her life.

She drew as a child and painted her first large work when she was 58 years old. But she was in her late 70s before she became serious with her oils, using her childhood experiences in such works as "Apple Pickers" and "Sugaring Off." Her first paintings were given away or sold for very little money. In 1939 Louis Caldor, an art collector, saw one of her paintings hanging in a drugstore window in Hoosick Falls, New York, so he drove to her farm and bought her entire stock of 15 paintings. Three of them were shown that year at the Museum of Modern Art in New York City and immediately her work was praised.

Grandma Moses created 2000 paintings in her style, which was lauded for its pure color, attention to detail, and innocent style (American primitive). She died at the age of 101.

With six aspects to the Midheaven, she captured the public's heart through Venus and through her attention to detail in Saturn. She spoke to us with her Mercury quintile the Midheaven. Her Moon quintile Neptune suggests a child's playground, which perhaps accounts for her innocent style.

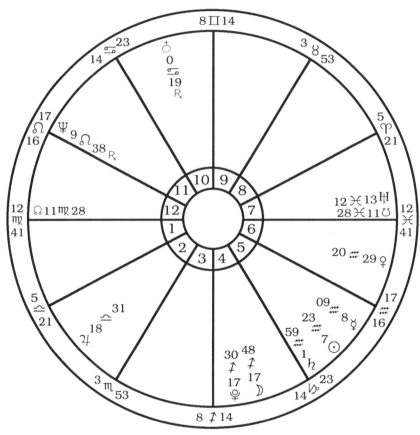

WOLFGANG AMADEUS MOZART
composer
January 27, 1756
8:00 P.M. L.M.T.
Salzburg, Austria
13E01 47N48
(*American Book of Charts*)

☽♀☌♀	☉☿◎♃
♂☌☊ASC	♂◎♃
♃☌♥	♂◎♅
	♂◎☋

COMMENTARY: Mozart's musical genius was evident at three years of age, and at four he wrote his first compositions. When he was six, his father, an excellent musician and his only teacher, took him and his sister, also a prodigy, on a tour of Europe, where they created a sensation.

In 1773 he entered the service of the prince-archbishop of Salzburg, with whom he became dissatisfied. He also disliked Salzburg, so he resigned and moved to Vienna to compose and perform on his own. He was in constant financial difficulty for the rest of his life. He supported himself by giving lessons and concerts and by the usually small amounts he received for his compositions.

Exhausted by years of privation, he died writing his own requiem, which had been commissioned by a mysterious dark stranger who, in actuality, was the servant of a Viennese nobleman who wanted to buy the requiem and pass it off as his own. But Mozart, ill and overworked, was convinced it was the messenger of death informing him of his own demise. He was buried in an unmarked pauper's grave.

Mozart excelled in every musical form of his time. He brought the musical forms of the eighteenth century to perfection and established models that have yet to be surpassed.

Every planet in Mozart's chart, with the exception of Saturn, is aspected in quintile and tredecile. His soaring imagination and sense of rapturous harmony is shown through Moon quintile Venus and Jupiter quintile Neptune. He had the ability to hear the music of the spheres.

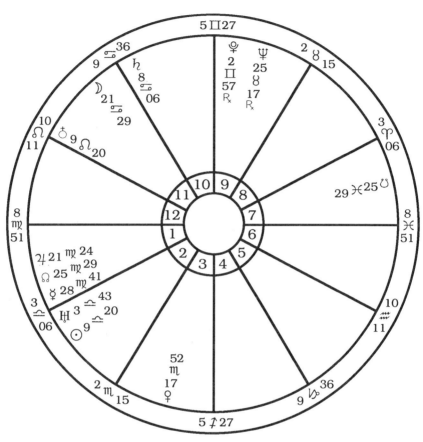

RUTH BRYAN OWEN
congresswoman
October 2, 1885
3:30 A.M. C.S.T.
Jacksonville, Illinois
90W14 39N44
(*Profiles of Women*, p. 197)

)Q⚷   ♃⊙♀
♀QASC   ☊⊙MC
☌Q♆
♃Q♄
☋QMC

COMMENTARY: Ruth Bryan Owen was immersed in politics, traveling on campaign trips at an early age with her father, William Jennings Bryan.

Her first marriage ended in divorce. In 1910 she married a British army officer, Major Reginald Owen. She served as a nurse in World War I and subsequently turned to public lecturing, advocating women's involvement in politics. She was charming and articulate.

After the death of her husband, she twice was elected as congresswoman from Florida, the first woman from Florida to achieve this position. She lost her bid in 1932 because she supported prohibition.

In his first term, Franklin Roosevelt appointed her minister to Denmark, the first woman even appointed to a United States diplomatic post. She resigned after her marriage to Captain Borge Rohde of the Danish Royal Guards but served as an alternate United States delegate to the United Nations Assembly.

Her Venus in the Third House quintiling her Ascendant would suggest her as a spokesperson for women in general, and with Jupiter quintile Saturn, politics would be a natural selection.

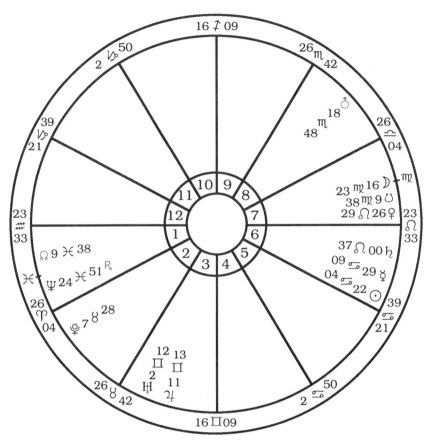

EMMELINE PANKHURST
feminist activist
July 14, 1858
9:30 P.M. L.M.T.
Manchester, England
2W15 53N20
(*Profiles of Women*, p. 115)

⊙♀♀   ☿♄⦵⦵♂
♀♉ASC   ♀⦵♀
           ♀⦵MC
           ♃⦵ASC

COMMENTARY: Coming from a home interested in reform movements, Emmeline Goulden married Richard Pankhurst, a lawyer who was a longtime advocate of social reform and women's suffrage.

In 1903, with her daughter, Christabel, and some friends, she founded the Woman's Social and Political Union, which became militant in 1905. In 1908 she was arrested and sentenced to three months in prison, thus firing up the movement. The feminist movement burst forth. They broke windows, destroyed property, and set fire to a railway station.

Emmeline Pankhurst accepted responsibility for these acts and on April 3, 1913, she was sentenced to three years in prison. Resorting to hunger strikes, she was released and rearrested many times until her final discharge on July 24. In 1914 she published *My Own Story*.

She and her group devoted all their energies to the national effort during World War I and regained the sympathy of those who were alienated by her group's militancy.

The Representation of the People Act was passed in June 1928, giving full suffrage to women (the 1919 passage granted voting rights to women over 30 years of age).

She was a candidate for Parliament upon her death in 1928. Today a bronze statue stands in the Victoria Tower Gardens near the Parliament in her honor. Her daughter, Sylvia, published her biography, *Life of Emmeline Pankhurst* in 1936.

With Venus tredecile Pluto and Mercury tredecile Mars, Pankhurst had the ammunition necessary to battle the forces that were repressing women's rights.

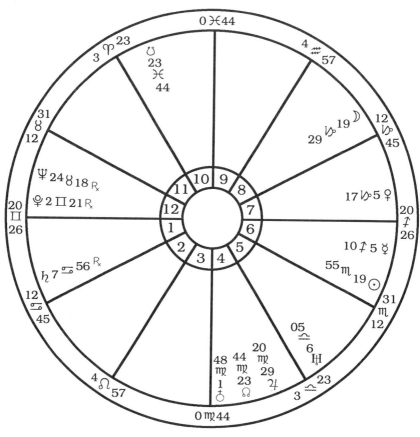

GEORGE PATTON
general
November 11, 1885
6:38 P.M. P.S.T.
San Marino, California
118W06 34N07
(*American Book of Charts*)

COMMENTARY: George Patton attended Virginia Military Institute in 1903, and after his graduation from the United States Military Academy, was commissioned a second lieutenant in the 15th Cavalry.

In 1916 he acted as aide to General John Pershing in the Mexican expedition and in 1917 went with Pershing to France as commander of his headquarters troops. In 1917 Patton was one of the first with the new tank corps and was assigned the duty of organizing and training the 1st Tank Brigade near Langres, France. He was subsequently awarded the Distinguished Service Cross and the Distinguished Service Medal and promoted to colonel.

In 1941 he was promoted to major general, and early in 1942 became commander of the 1st Armored Corps, which he trained in the desert near Indio, California. He played a major role in the invasion of North Africa in the Second World War. He helped clear Sicily in 38 days, a victory diminished by an incident in which he struck a hospital patient being treated for shell shock. He apologized publicly. Shortly before the invasion of Europe, he was reprimanded by General Eisenhower for indiscreet political remarks.

Omar Bradley, remarking on one of Patton's brilliant military maneuvers during the war, called it "one of the most astonishing feats of generalship of our campaign in the west..." [10]

Patton eventually was promoted to four-star general. Due to his outspoken comments on denazification policies, he was assigned to a small headquarters. He died in an automobile accident in Mannheim, Germany, shortly afterward.

His Moon tredecile Jupiter gave him the ability to instinctively know the larger pattern, to know how the other person might plan their strategy. His Mercury aspecting the Nodes could indicate his place in history as an outspoken critic.

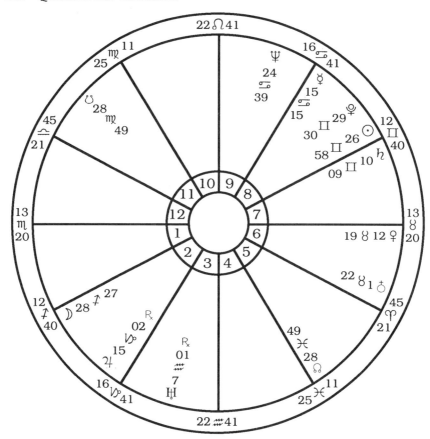

SYLVIA PORTER
financial columnist
June 18, 1913
3:50 P.M. E.S.T.
New York, New York
73W57 40N45
(*Profiles of Women*, p. 92)

☿ Q ♂	☿ ◉ ☊
☿ Q ☋	♂ ◉ ♃
♀ Q ♆	♃ ◉ ☋
♃ Q ☊	♄ ◉ ☋
♄ Q ☊	♆ ◉ ASC
♄ Q MC	

COMMENTARY: *Sylvia Porter's New Money Book for the 80s* made Sylvia Porter the best-known economic adviser in America. Overcoming prejudice in a male-oriented field, she had 40,000,000 readers for her syndicated column entitled "Sylvia Porter," which is well respected by politicians, economists, and businesspeople. Energetic, clear, and humorous, her writing also is personal, with such phrases as "You have to understand" and "You have to care."

She was born into a secure middle-class family who encouraged her to think. The family moved to Brooklyn during her childhood, where her father practiced medicine. In 1925, when she was 12, he died suddenly of a heart attack. That plus the stock market crash of 1929 were events that she later regarded as major influences on her life.

In the beginning she concealed her identity as a woman by writing under the name of S. F. Porter. In 1935 the *New York Post* hired her to write an occasional financial column. Soon she had a daily column first called "Financial Post Marks" and later "S. F. Porter Says." Her credibility grew and in 1962 she was named by President Kennedy to the Consumer Advisory Council.

After thirty years with the *New York Post*, she switched to the *New York Daily News* in 1978. Her column is syndicated in 450 newspapers around the world and she has received many awards.

Her vigorous writing is shown by Mercury quintile Mars. With Mars tredecile Jupiter   and Jupiter and Saturn aspecting the Nodes, she has a prophetic business sense.

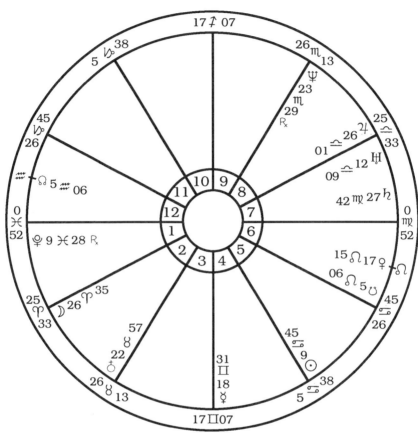

GEORGE SAND
(LUCIE AURORE DUPIN DUDEVANT)
writer
July 1, 1804
10:25 P.M. L.M.T.
Paris, France
2E20 48N50
(*Profiles of Women*, p. 105)

☽Q☉   ☽⊘♀
♂Q♀   ☉⊘♃
♆Q☊   ☿⊘ASC
           ♆⊘☊

COMMENTARY: Lucie Dupin followed the traditional pattern of her time and dutifully married Baron Dudevant at the age of 18. They had two children, and eight years later, she left him. The next five years were those of "romantic rebellion." She lived a wild life in Paris, associating with artists, smoking cigars, wearing men's clothing, and flaunting every custom of the time. She published a few stories in collaboration with Jules Sandeau, signing them J. Sand. Her first independent novel was published under her famous pseudonym, George Sand.

Her tempestuous affair with Alfred de Musset, six years younger than she, may have been the "wildest love affair of the century." They separated and her next affair was with Frederic Chopin who, afflicted with tuberculosis, brought out "the mother complex in her (her children have been called the greatest love of her life)." [11]

"She then transferred to the people the powers of love that she had been squandering on men." [12] She began to write social and humanitarian novels. As she grew older, her novels covered country life and the gentry.

Though her life was tumultuous, her passion and depressions always were overridden by an innate optimism. She was remembered as kindhearted and caring, a woman with an "undefinable aura of aristocratic prestige, taste, and beauty." [13]

Her powers of love are certainly emphasized in her Moon tredecile Venus, and her "undefinable aura of aristocratic prestige, taste, and beauty" shows in that same Moon tredecile Sun as well as the Sun tredecile Jupiter.

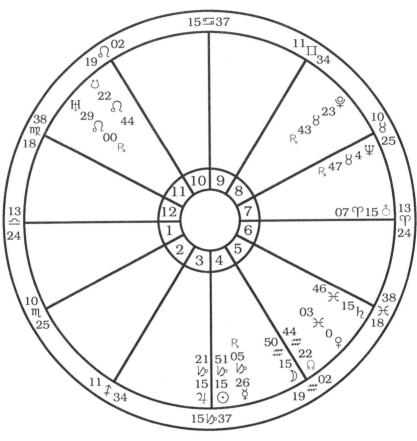

CARL SANDBERG
writer
January 6, 1878
00:05 A.M. L.M.T.
Galesburg, Illinois
90W23 40N57
(*American Book of Charts*)

ΨⓆMC   ☉♃☽Ψ
           ☿☽MPΨ♀

COMMENTARY: Carl Sandberg grew up in a small prairie town where Abraham Lincoln and Stephen Douglas had one of their historic debates in 1858. He grew up hearing those tales.

Sandberg had to leave school at age 13 and go to work. His first job was driving a milk wagon, during which time he would recite pieces of literature. He also worked as a bootblack and porter in a local barber shop where he heard customers talk about history and politics.

He was a war correspondent during the Spanish-American War and received free tuition to Lombard College for his services. Around examination time, however, he left and never graduated. He was a true hobo, taking jobs at various newspapers and wandering about the country getting to know farmhands, river men, and black stevedores.

In 1908 he married Lillian Steichen while working for the *Milwaukee Journal and Daily News* to support his new family. In 1916 his *Chicago Poems* was published followed by *Cornhuskers* in 1918 which won the Poetry Society Prize. He eventually published a 6-volume work on Abraham Lincoln, part of which won the Pulitzer Prize for history in 1940. Many more works were published during his life.

Carl Sandberg is regarded as the poet of the prairie. Much of his work celebrated industrial and agricultural America. With his Sun, Mercury, and Jupiter tredecile Neptune, we can see why he was called "the Poet of the Prairie."

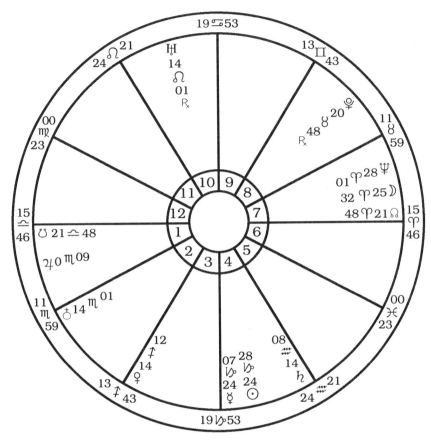

ALBERT SCHWEITZER
humanitarian
January 14, 1875
11:50 P.M. L.M.T.
Kayserburg, Alsace
7E16 48N09
(*American Book of Charts*)

☽ ♆ ☊ ♀ ♄	☽ ♆ ☊ Ⓜ ♅
☉ ☿ ♀ ♂	♄ Ⓜ ☊
♅ ♀ ☋	MP ♂ ♃ Ⓜ MC

COMMENTARY: Albert Schweitzer began piano lessons at the age of five. Although he found schoolwork difficult, he pushed himself to achieve in the most difficult subjects. He attended theology school and received a scholarship to study philosophy at Sorbonne. As curator of St. Nicholas Church, he devoted much time to charitable work.

He decided that after age 30 he would devote himself to others, so from 1905 to 1922 he studied medicine. After receiving his M.D., he studied tropical diseases in preparation for the medical missionary work he wanted to do in Africa.

Schweitzer spent much of his life in Lambarene, French Equatorial Africa, where he built his hospital of 50 buildings, many of which he built with his own hands. His hospital standards, although appearing primitive, were in reality very high.

Among his published works were an authoritative biography, *Johann Sebastian Bach*, and *The Quest of the Historical Jesus* and *Civilization and Ethics*. After 1924 he spent his time between his hospital and lecture tours of Europe. In 1928 he received the Goethe Prize of 10,000 marks and was awarded the 1952 Nobel Peace Prize.

With Moon tredecile Uranus, Schweitzer had a deep emotional commitment and need to nurture all people regardless of origin. World recognition of his untiring efforts and encompassing philosophy is revealed in the Mars and Jupiter tredecile the Midheaven aspects.

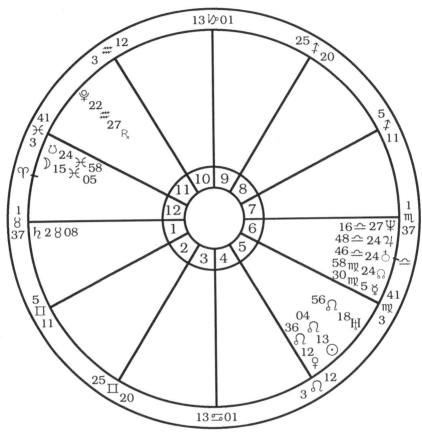

PERCY BYSSHE SHELLEY
poet
August 4, 1792
10:00 P.M. L.M.T.
Horsham, England
0W20 51N03
(*American Book of Charts*)

☉♀♇♂♃Ψ ASC☽MC
♀♇♄ASC ☊☽MC
          ♄ASC☽♅

COMMENTARY: Percy Bysshe Shelley was born on his family's estate in Sussex. He attended Eton and Oxford, from which he was thrown out for writing a pamphlet entitled *The Necessity of Atheism*.

Shortly thereafter he married Harriet Westbrook, but within three years he had eloped with Mary Godwin, later to be the author of *Frankenstein*. They were married after Harriet's suicide in 1816.

On July 8, 1822, Shelley drowned when his boat went down during a storm off the coast of Italy. He was 29 years old.

Shelley is called one of the greatest of the English romantic poets, a group including Keats and Byron. He was an avid champion of freedom and expounded upon the topic in his great work, *Prometheus Unbound*. Shelly had an "ability to write highly musical verse, an ability he also displayed in many lyric poems, among the most famous of which are 'Ode to the West Wind,' 'The Skylark,' 'The Triumph of Life,' and 'Adonis,' an elegy on the death of John Keats." [14]

"His abilities were unusual. In England at that time, probably only Samuel Taylor Coleridge was his superior in learning and reading, and his equal in comprehending and simplifying great subjects." [15]

But, of course, Shelly died when he was 29.

What might he have accomplished if he had lived a longer life? His ability to simplify great subjects is perhaps indicated by Saturn quintile Pluto, and his lyric poetry by Venus quintile Neptune.

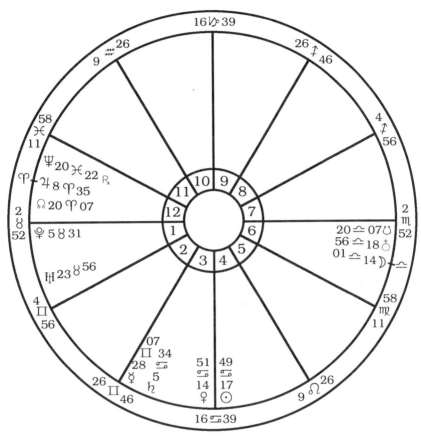

NIKOLA TESLA
scientist, inventor, genius
July 9/10, 1856
12:00 midnight L.M.T.
Smiljan, Yugoslavia
15E19 44N35
(*American Book of Charts*)

☉♀♇♀ASC ☽♂☽☿
        ♀ASC☽MC

COMMENTARY: Nikola Tesla's mother, Georgina Mandic, was also an inventor, as was her father. He spent four years at the Polytechnic School in Graz, where he specialized in mathematics, physics, and mechanics. He then spent two years studying philosophy at the University of Prague.

In Budapest in 1881 he developed his first electrical invention, a telephone repeater, and gave birth to his idea of a rotating magnetic field.

He moved to the United States in 1884 and became a citizen. He was associated with Edison for a while but then established his own laboratory in New York City. Stories have come down about how the police station in his neighborhood received constant calls about strange happenings and noises which the police eventually attributed to Tesla at work in his laboratory.

He invented many things; among the best known was his "epoch-making" alternating current motors and his Tesla coil or transformer.

An outstanding genius, Tesla indulged in fantastic ideas toward the end of his life. When he was 78, for instance, he claimed he had invented a death beam that could destroy 10,000 airplanes at a distance of 250 miles, and could also wipe out an army of 1,000,000 people instantly.

His indulgence in fantastic ideas and his ability to give some of them form shows in his Saturn tredecile Neptune. His Moon tredecile Mercury gave him conscious access to his subconscious storehouse of information, and Mercury tredecile Mars implies the mechanical ability.

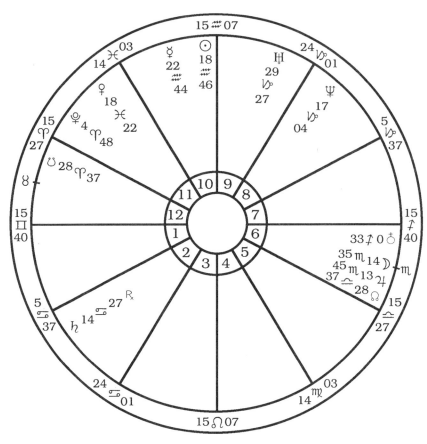

JULES VERNE
science fiction writer
February 8, 1828
12:00 noon L.M.T.
Nantes, France
1W33 47N13
(*American Book of Charts*)

☽♃♀♅   ☉♍♌
☉♀☋   ♀♍♂
♂♀MC

COMMENTARY: After studying law in Paris, Verne spent most of his time in literary and theatrical activities. Alexander Dumas supported his first successful play in 1850. In 1863, his book, *Five Weeks in a Balloon*, brought him public acclaim, prompting a series of incredible romances about invention and science. Thus he became the first novelist of modern science fiction.

Some of what he drew from the fertile fields of his imagination has become fact. In *Nautilus*, his submarine predates by twenty-five years the first successful power submarine. *From the Earth to the Moon* was prophetic of the the development of spaceship travel one hundred years later.

He averaged more than one novel a year for over forty years on a variety of different subjects. One of his most popular and successful novels was *Around the World in Eighty Days*, published in 1873.

Certainly his Moon and Jupiter quintile Uranus indicate his ability to forsee the future and to imagine the technical expertise required to produce some of the machinery, such as the power submarine and the spaceship in his novels. With Pluto in the Eleventh House quintile his Ascendant, he understood the power source of the future.

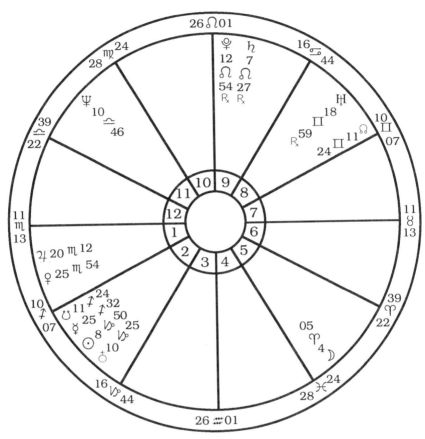

DIANE VON FURSTENBERG
entrepreneur
December 31, 1946
3:00 A.M. M.E.T.
Brussels, Belgium
4E20 50N50
(*Profiles of Women*, p. 282)

☽ Q ♅   ♀ ⑩ ♄
☿ Q ♆   ♀ ⑩ MC
☊ Q MC

COMMENTARY: Diane von Furstenberg is known as "the designer who put dresses back on women." She nurtured a one-woman operation into a multimillion dollar business marketing a variety of products. The "diane dress," a simple shirtdress in geometric print, was the cornerstone of her fashion empire. She said, "I never pretended I was a fabulous designer. I am a woman who makes clothes." Her philosophy is to "simplify everything."

Her mother, who spent fourteen months in a Nazi concentration camp during World War II, taught her independence and self-confidence. She went to finishing schools and attended the University of Madrid, but transferred to the University of Geneva the following year and studied economics. There she met Prince Eduard Egon von Furstenberg, heir to the Fiat fortune. His family disapproved--their lineage goes back several hundred years-- but they were married in Paris in 1969 in a dress she designed herself. They have two children and are now divorced.

She runs a tight schedule, beginning with exercise at 7:30 A.M. She oversees all aspects of her empire. Being a good mother is important to her and she takes her responsibilities seriously.

Her own description of herself as a woman who makes clothes, especially a simple shirtdress with geometric designs, is an apt description of her Venus tredecile Saturn. With the Moon quintile Uranus, she still has an electric touch on the pulse of the public.

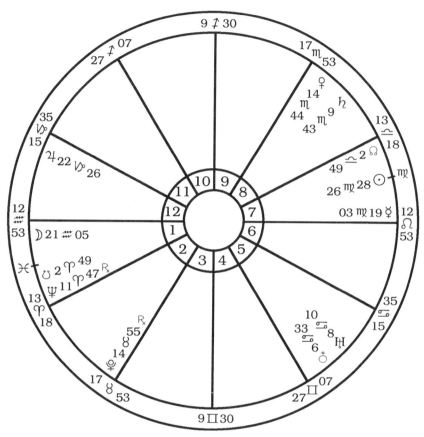

H.G. WELLS
writer, prognosticator
September 21, 1866
4:30 P.M. L.M.T.
Bromley, England
0E01 51N25
(*American Book of Charts*)

☿♈☌♅   ♃☍♌
☉♈MC
♃♈♄
♃♈☊

COMMENTARY: Herbert George Wells was an omnivorous reader. He began this habit when he was eight years old and immobilized for some time with a broken leg.

He spent some time as a draper's assistant, after which he taught in a private school for a year. He won a scholarship to the Normal School of Science in South Kensington in 1884. He lost interest and left without a degree, teaching in private school for four years, and finally getting his B.S. in 1890.

In 1891 he was in London teaching in a correspondence school and married to his cousin Isabel. He wrote on educational subjects. But his sensational literary career began with the publication of *The Time Machine* in 1895. He divorced his wife and married a student, Amy Catherine Robbins, in 1895.

His incredible writing career continued with *The Island of Dr. Moreau* in 1896, *The Invisible Man* in 1897, *The War of the Worlds* in 1898, *The First Men in the Moon* in 1901, and *The War in the Air* in 1908.

Wells grew dissatisfied with this kind of writing and began expressing his hostility to the victorian social order. He met George Bernard Shaw, who claimed that he and Wells had changed the mind of Europe. He continued to write on a variety of subjects for the remainder of his life.

We can see the aggressive writing in Mercury quintile Mars and the futuristic touch in Mercury quintile Uranus. Jupiter quintile Saturn suggests his concern with the political and social structure of the day.

Personality Compilations by Aspect

Moon quintile Sun:

Victor Hugo
Jane Austen
Charlotte Bronte
George Sand
Elizabeth Arden

Moon tredecile Sun:

Helen Keller
Mary Shelley
Margaret Chase Smith

Moon quintile Mercury:

Jean Houston
Marcel Proust
Margaret Mead

Moon tredecile Mercury:

Albert Einstein
Nikola Tesla

Moon quintile Venus:

Wolfgang Mozart
Victor Hugo
Abraham Lincoln

Moon tredecile Venus:

George Sand
Margaret Chase Smith

Moon quintile Mars:

Friedrich Nietzsche

Moon tredecile Mars:

Sigmund Freud
Ernest Hemingway
Jimi Hendrix
Margaret Chase Smith

Moon quintile Jupiter:

Albert Einstein
Sigmund Freud
Gloria Steinem
Mary Baker Eddy

Moon tredecile Jupiter:

Mark Edmund Jones
Elvis Presley
John Lennon
Friedrich Nietzsche
Charlotte Bronte
George Patton
Chris Evert

Moon quintile Saturn:

Jean Houston
Albert Schweitzer

Moon tredecile Saturn:

Albert Einstein
Victor Hugo
John Lennon
Herman Melville

Bela Lugosi
Giuseppe Verdi
Emily Bronte
Cynthia Gregory
Margaret Chase Smith

Moon quintile Uranus:

Jules Verne
Diane von Furstenberg
Margaret Mead
Ruth Bryan Owen

Moon tredecile Uranus:

Albert Schweitzer
Martin Luther
Edouard Manet
Gloria Steinem
Chris Evert
Margaret Chase Smith

Moon quintile Neptune:

Friedrich Nietzsche
Grandma Moses

Moon tredecile Neptune:

Cher

Moon quintile Pluto:

Victor Hugo
Elizabeth Arden
Clara Barton
Margaret Chase Smith

Moon tredecile Pluto:

Florence Entwistle

Moon quintile North Node:

George Eliot
Helen Keller
Ruth Bryan Owen

Moon tredecile North Node:

Edith Cavell
Margaret Mead
Maria Montessori

Moon quintile South Node:

Edith Cavell
Margaret Mead
Maria Montessori

Moon tredecile South Node:

Helen Keller
Ruth Bryan Owen

Moon quintile Ascendant:

Gelsey Kirkland

Sun tredecile Venus:

Not possible

Sun quintile Mars:

Albert Schweitzer
Percy Bysshe Shelley

Sun tredecile Mars:

Adrienne Hirt

Sun quintile Jupiter:

Percy Bysshe Shelley
Alice Bailey
George Eliot
Maria Montessori
Margaret Chase Smith

Sun tredecile Jupiter:

Wolfgang Mozart
George Sand
Clara Barton

Sun quintile Saturn:

Charlotte Bronte
Helen Keller
Gelsey Kirkland
Abraham Lincoln

Sun tredecile Saturn:

Clara Barton

Sun quintile Uranus:

Elton John
Alice Bailey

Sun tredecile Uranus:

Abraham Lincoln
Amelia Earhart
Elisabeth Kübler-Ross

Sun quintile Neptune:

Bruce Lee
Percy Bysshe Shelley
Gloria Allred
Gelsey Kirkland
Abraham Lincoln

Sun tredecile Neptune:

Elizabeth Barrett Browning
Carl Sandberg
Agatha Christie
Helen Frankenthaler
Indira Gandhi

Sun quintile Pluto:

John Lennon
Nikola Tesla
Jean Houston
Emmeline Pankhurst

Sun tredecile Pluto:

Agatha Christie
Billie Jean King
Maria Montessori
Gloria Steinem

Sun quintile NorthNode:

Gloria Allred

Sun tredecile North Node:

  Billie Jean King
  Jules Verne
  Abraham Lincoln

Sun quintile South Node:

  Billie Jean King
  Jules Verne
  Abraham Lincoln

Sun tredecile South Node:

  Gloria Allred

Sun quintile Ascendant:

  Nikola Tesla

Sun tredecile Ascendant:

  Albert Einstein

Sun quintile MC:

  Steve Allen
  John Lennon
  H. G. Wells
  Abraham Lincoln
  George Eliot
  Jules Verne
  Grandma Moses

Sun tredecile MC:

Elvis Presley

Mercury quintile Venus:

  Clara Bow

Mercury tredecile Venus:

  Not possible

Mercury quintile Mars:

  Francoise Gauguelin
  Charlotte Bronte
  Albert Schweitzer
  H. G. Wells
  Maria Montessori
  Sylvia Porter
  Agatha Christie

Mercury tredecile Mars:

  Nikola Tesla
  Emmeline Pankhurst

Mercury quintile Jupiter:

  Doris Chase Doane

Mercury tredecile Jupiter:

  Wolfgang Mozart
  Agatha Christie
  Mary Baker Eddy

Mercury quintile Saturn:

Alice Bailey
Jane Fonda

Mercury tredecile Saturn:

Taylor Caldwell
Mary Baker Eddy

Mercury quintile Uranus:

Charles Lindberg
H. G. Wells
Indira Gandhi
Maria Montessori

Mercury tredecile Uranus:

Helen Frankenthaler

Mercury quintile Neptune:

Francoise Gauguelin
Taylor Caldwell
Diane von Furstenberg
Jane Austen

Mercury tredecile Neptune:

Elizaberth Barrett Browning
Carl Sandberg
Helen Frankenthaler

Mercury quintile Pluto:

Helen Keller

Mercury tredecile Pluto:

Carl Sandberg

Mercury quintile North Node:

Edith Cavell
George Patton

Mercury tredecile North Node:

Elizabeth Arden
Jane Austen
Sylvia Porter

Mercury quintile South Node:

Elizabeth Arden
Jane Austen
Sylvia Porter

Mercury tredecile South Node:

Edith Cavell
George Patton

Mercury quintile Ascendant:

Jane Austen

Mercury tredecile Ascendant:

George Sand
Clara Barton
Helen Keller

Mercury quintile MC:

Steve Allen

Grandma Moses

Mercury tredecile MC:

Isabelle Pagan

Venus quintile Mars:

Alan Alda
Percy Bysshe Shelley
Jane Fonda
Jane Austen

Venus tredecile Mars:

Jules Verne

Venus quintile Jupiter:

Elvis Presley
Percy Bysshe Shelley
Elizabeth Arden

Venus tredecile Jupiter:

John Lennon
Ernest Hemingway
Elisabeth Kübler-Ross
Chris Evert

Venus quintile Saturn:

Karl Marx

Venus tredecile Saturn:

John Lennon

Diane von Furstenberg
Billie Jean King

Venus quintile Uranus:

Elisabeth Kübler-Ross

Venus tredecile Uranus:

Chris Evert

Venus quintile Neptune:

Percy Bysshe Shelley
Sylvia Porter
Elisabeth Kübler-Ross

Venus tredecile Neptune:

Elizabeth Barrett Browning
Florence Entwistle
Maria Montessori

Venus quintile Pluto:

Wolfgang Mozart
Nikola Tesla

Venus tredecile Pluto:

Emmeline Pankhurst
Margaret Rhea Seddon
Florence Entwistle

Venus quintile North Node:

Jackie Robinson

Albert Einstein

Emmeline Pankhurst
Uri Geller

Venus tredecile North Node:

Mars quintile Jupiter:

Katherine Mansfield
Mary Shelley

Gelsey Kirkland

Venus quintile South Node:

Mars tredecile Jupiter:

Katherine Mansfield
Mary Shelley

Wolfgang Mozart
Van Cliburn
Sylvia Porter

Venus tredecile South Node:

Helen Gahagan Douglas
Florence Entwistle

Jackie Robinson
Albert Einstein

Mars quintile Saturn:

Venus quintile Ascendant:

Ada Byron
Amelia Earhart

Prince Charles
Emily Bronte
Nikola Tesla
Elizabeth Arden
Florence Entwistle
Ruth Bryan Owen

Mars tredecile Saturn:

Louis Pasteur
Helen Keller
Agatha Christie
Emmeline Pankhurst
Lois M. Rodden

Venus tredecile Ascendant:

Elisabeth Kübler-Ross
Billie Jean King

Mars quintile Uranus:

Venus quintile MC:

Ernest Hemingway
Marcel Proust
Amelia Earhart
Jane Fonda

Mary Baker Eddy

Venus tredecile MC:

Mars tredecile Uranus:

Grandma Moses

Wolfgang Mozart

Mars quintile Neptune:

Ruth Bryan Owen

Mars tredecile Neptune:

Elizabeth Barrett Browning
Johannes Kepler
Elizabeth Arden
Billie Jean King

Mars quintile Pluto:

Louis Pasteur
Alice Bailey
George Sand
Mary Baker Eddy
Helen Keller

Mars tredecile Pluto:

Grandma Moses

Mars quintile North Node:

Wolfgang Amadeus Mozart
Mary Shelley

Mars tredecile North Node:

Emmeline Pankhurst
George Sand

Mars quintile South Node:

Emmeline Pankhurst
George Sand

Mars tredecile South Node:

Wolfgang Amadeus Mozart
Mary Shelley

Mars quintile Ascendant:

Hugo Black
George Patton
Emily Bronte
Wolfgang Mozart

Mars tredecile Ascendant:

Johannes Kepler
Chris Evert
Helen Keller

Mars quintile MC:

Jules Verne

Mars tredecile MC:

Winston Churchill
Ernest Hemingway
Gloria Allred
Albert Schweitzer

Jupiter quintile Saturn:

Emily Bronte
H. G. Wells
Amelia Earhart
Ruth Bryan Owen

Jupiter tredecile Saturn:

Charlotte Bronte
Winston Churchill
Chris Evert
Abraham Lincoln

Jupiter quintile Uranus:

Jules Verne
Amelia Earhart
Ruth Bryan Owen
Billie Jean King

Jupiter tredecile Uranus:

Clara Barton
Indira Gandhi

Jupiter quintile Neptune:

Albert Einstein
Wolfgang Mozart
Emmeline Pankhurst

Jupiter tredecile Neptune:

Carl Sandberg
Gloria Allred
Clara Barton
Margaret Chase Smith
Abraham Lincoln

Jupiter quintile Pluto:

Isabelle Pagan

Jupiter tredecile Pluto:

Ruth Bryan Owen

Margaret Rhea Seddon

Jupiter quintile North Node:

Edith Cavell
Sylvia Porter

Jupiter tredecile North Node:

Gloria Allred
Margaret Chase Smith
H. G. Wells

Jupiter quintile South Node:

Gloria Allred
Margaret Chase Smith
H. G. Wells

Jupiter tredecile South Node:

Edith Cavell
Sylvia Porter

Jupiter quintile Ascendant:

Cynthia Gregory
Mary Shelley

Jupiter tredecile Ascendant:

Emmeline Pankhurst

Jupiter quintile MC:

Margaret Chase Smith
Jean Houston
Jane Fonda

Jupiter tredecile MC:

Winston Churchill
Clara Barton
Agatha Christie
Uri Geller
Abraham Lincoln
Albert Schweitzer

Saturn quintile Uranus:

Florence Entwistle

Saturn tredecile Uranus:

Francoise Gauguelin
Louis Pasteur
New York Stock Exchange
Percy Bysshe Shelley
Clara Barton
Chris Evert

Saturn quintile Neptune:

Albert Schweitzer
Cynthia Gregory

Saturn tredecile Neptune:

Johann von Goethe
Marcel Proust
Clara Barton
Helen Frankenthaler
Nikola Tesla

Saturn quintile Pluto:

Marc Edmund Jones

Percy Bysshe Shelley

Saturn tredecile Pluto:

Ellen Glasgow

Saturn quintile North Node:

Amelia Earhart
Sylvia Porter
Albert Schweitzer
Ruth Bryan Owen

Saturn tredecile North Node:

Alice Bailey
Helen Keller
Gelsey Kirkland
Jackie Robinson

Saturn quintile South Node:

Alice Bailey
Helen Keller
Gelsey Kirkland
Jackie Robinson

Saturn tredecile South Node:

Amelia Earhart
Ruth Bryan Owen
Sylvia Porter
Albert Schweitzer

Saturn quintile Ascendant:

Abraham Lincoln

Saturn tredecile Ascendant:

Marcel Proust
Elizabeth Arden

Saturn quintile MC:

Sylvia Porter
Grandma Moses

Saturn tredecile MC:

Isabel Pagan
Charlotte Bronte
Clara Barton
Edith Cavell
Agatha Christie

Uranus quintile Neptune:

Grandma Moses
Emmeline Pankhurst

Uranus tredecile Neptune:

Jane Austen
Albert Schweitzer
Winston Churchill
Cynthia Gregory
Margaret Rhea Seddon

Uranus quintile Pluto:

Jean Houston
Billie Jean King

Uranus tredecile Pluto:

Helen Frankenthaler
Elisabeth Kübler-Ross

Uranus quintile North Node:

Amelia Earhart
Jackie Robinson
Jane Austen
Billie Jean King

Uranus tredecile North Node:

Edith Cavell
Winston Churchill
George Eliot
Elisabeth Kübler-Ross
Albert Schweitzer

Uranus quintile South Node:

Edith Cavell
Winston Churchill
George Eliot
Elisabeth Kübler-Ross
Albert Schweitzer

Uranus tredecile South Node:

Jane Austen
Amelia Earhart
Jackie Robinson
Billie Jean King

Uranus quintile Ascendant:

Mary Shelley

Uranus tredecile Ascendant:

Abraham Lincoln
George Patton
Percy Bysshe Shelley
Jane Austen

Uranus quintile MC:

John Lennon
Helen Frankenthaler
Mary Baker Eddy

Uranus tredecile MC:

Alexander Graham Bell
USA (with 7 Sagittarius rising)
Gloria Steinem

Neptune quintile Pluto:

Louisa May Alcott

Neptune tredecile Pluto:

George Sand
Mary Shelley

Neptune quintile North Node

Jane Fonda
George Sand
Carl Sandberg

Neptune tredecile North Node:

Gelsey Kirkland

Cynthia Gregory

Neptune quintile South Node:

Gelsey Kirkland
Cynthia Gregory

Neptune tredecile South Node:

Jane Fonda
George Sand
Carl Sandberg

Neptune quintile Ascendant:

Bruce Lee
Ernest Hemingway
Abraham Lincoln

Neptune tredecile Ascendant:

Johann von Goethe
Sylvia Porter
Billie Jean King

Neptune quintile MC:

Carl Sandberg
Indira Gandhi
Mary Baker Eddy
Uri Geller
Jackie Robinson

Neptune tredecile MC:

Elisabeth Kübler-Ross
Mary Shelley

Pluto quintile North Node:

Florence Entwistle

Pluto tredecile North Node:

Mary Shelley
Ruth Bryan Owen
George Patton

Pluto quintile South Node:

Mary Shelley
Ruth Bryan Owen
George Patton

Pluto tredecile South Node:

Florence Entwistle

Pluto quintile Ascendant:

Uri Geller
Percy Bysshe Shelley
Alice Bailey
Emmeline Pankhurst
Jules Verne

Pluto tredecile Ascendant:

Gloria Steinem
Grandma Moses

Pluto quintile MC:

Albert Einstein

Pluto tredecile MC:

Sigmund Freud
Nikola Tesla

North Node quintile Ascendant:

Agatha Christie
Mary Baker Eddy

North Node tredecile Ascendant:

Helen Frankenthaler
Abraham Lincoln
Jackie Robinson

North Node quintile MC:

Diane von Furstenberg
Maria Montessori
Grandma Moses

North Node tredecile MC:

Ruth Bryan Owen
Jules Verne
Mary Shelley
Percy Bysshe Shelley

South Node quintile Ascendant:

Helen Frankenthaler
Abraham Lincoln

South Node tredecile Ascendant:

Agatha Christie
Mary Baker Eddy

South Node quintile MC:

Ruth Bryan Owen
Jules Verne

South Node tredecile MC:

Diane von Furstenberg
Maria Montessori
Grandma Moses
George Patton
Nikola Tesla

Ascendant quintille MC:

Helen Gahagan Douglas
Abraham Lincoln

Ascendant tredecile MC:

Percy Bysshe Shelley
Nikola Tesla

Sources of Charts

Dictionary of American Biographies, vol. XIX, p. 509. New York: Charles Scribner and Sons, 1936.

Stephen Erlewine, *The Circle Book of Charts*. Ann Arbor, Mich.: Circle Books, 1972. (215 South State Street, 48108).

The Golden Home and High School Encyclopedia, vol. 4. New York: Golden Press, 1961.

Lois M. Rodden, *The American Book of Charts*. San Diego: Astro Computing Services, 1980. (P.O. Box 16430, 92116).

Lois M. Rodden, *Profiles of Women*. Tempe, Ariz.: American Federation of Astrologers, Inc., 1979.

Footnotes

[1] Lois M. Rodden, *The American Book of Charts*. San Diego: Astro Computing Services, 1980, p. 107. (P.O. Box 16430, 92116.)

[2] *Ibid.*, p. 107.

[3] *Encyclopedia Americana*, vol. 2. New York: Americana Corporation, 1966, p. 560.

[4] The editors of *Life*, "The Unforgettable Winston Churchill." New York: Time, Inc., 1965, p. 3.

[5] *Ibid.*, p. 126.

[6] *Encyclopedia Americana*, vol. 9, p. 577.

[7] *Ibid.*, vol. 10, p. 42A.

[8] *American Book of Charts*.

[9] Lois M. Rodden, *Profiles of Women*. Tempe, Ariz.: American Federation of Astrologers, Inc., 1979, p. 261.

[10] *Encyclopedia Americana*, vol. 21, p. 411.

[11] *Ibid.*, p. 250.

[12] *Ibid.*, p.250.

[13] *Ibid.*, p. 250.

[14] *The Golden Home and High School Encyclopedia*, vol. 16. New York: Golden Press, 1961, p. 2294.

[15] *Encyclopedia Americana*, vol. 24, p. 690.

Suggested Reading List

Dusty Bunker, *Numerology and Your Future*. West Chester, Pa.: Whitford Press, 1980.

Dusty Bunker, *Numerology, Astrology, and Dreams*. West Chester, Pa.: Whitford Press, 1988.

Keith Critchlow, *Time Stands Still*. New York: St. Martin's Press, 1982.

Gyorgy Doczi, *The Power of Limits*. Boulder, Co.: Shambhala Publications Inc. (80302), 1981.

Martin Gardner, *The Numerology of Dr. Matrix*. New York: Simon and Schuster, 1967.

Corinne Heline, *Sacred Science of Numbers*. La Canada, Calif.: New Age Press, Inc. (4636 Vineta Avenue, 91011), 1971.

S.K. Heninger, Jr., *Touches of Sweet Harmony: Pythagorean Cosmology and Renaissance Poetics*. San Marino, Calif.: The Huntington Library, 1974.

Paul Higgins, *Hermetic Masonry*. New York: Pyramid Publishing Company, 1916; Ferndale, Mi.: Trismegistus Press, 1980.

H.E. Huntley, *The Divine Proportion: A Study in Mathematical Beauty*. New York: Dover Publications, 1970.

Faith Javane and Dusty Bunker, *Numerology and the Divine Triangle*. West Chester, Pa.: Whitford Press, 1980.

"Geometry and Architecture" in *The Lindisfarne Letter*, volume 10. West Stockbridge, Mass.: The Lindisfarne Association, 1980.

"Homage to Pythagoras" in *The Lindisfarne Letter*, volume 14. West Stockbridge, Mass.: The Lindisfarne Association, 1982.

George Oliver, *The Pythagorean Triangle* (part of *Secret Doctrine Reference Series*). Minneapolis: Wizard's Book Shelf, 1975.

Nigel Pennick, *Sacred Geometry*. Wellingborough, Northampton-shire, England: Turnstone Press Limited, 1980.

L. Gordon Plummer, *The Mathematics of the Cosmic Mind*. Wheaton, Ill.: The Theosophical Publishing House, 1970.

Kenneth Sylvan Guthrie (compiler and translator), *The Pythagorean Sourcebook and Library*. Grand Rapids: Phanes Press (P.O. Box 6114, 49516), 1987.

Lionel Stebbing, *The Secrets of Numbers*. London: New Knowledge Books, 1963.

Thomas Taylor, *The Theoretic Arithmetic of the Pythagoreans*. New York: Samuel Weiser, 1978. Originally printed in London in 1816.

Barbara Walker, *Woman's Encyclopedia of Myths and Secrets*. New York: Harper and Row, Publishers Inc., 1983.